61
Gems
on Highway 61 MINNESOTA 61

A GUIDE TO MINNESOTA'S NORTH SHORE
From Well-Known Attractions to Best-Kept Secrets

by Kathryn Mayo and William Mayo

Adventure Publications, Inc.
Cambridge, Minnesota

Acknowledgments

We want to acknowledge our families, as always, as the source of meaning for our lives in this world. We are so grateful for the goodness we receive from those that love us no matter what. That kind of debt can never be truly repaid. The best we can do here is remember those dear to us and pass this hope and love on to our children. All of our relatives are here in our words, in our attempt at communicating the beauty of this place we love, the North Shore of Lake Superior.

All photos by William Mayo except the footer images by Dan Lynch.

Cover and book design by Jonathan Norberg

Edited by Brett Ortler

10 9 8 7 6 5 4 3 2 1

Copyright 2009 by Kathryn Mayo and William Mayo
Published by Adventure Publications, Inc.
820 Cleveland St. S
Cambridge, MN 55008
1-800-678-7006
www.adventurepublications.net
All rights reserved
Printed in China
ISBN-13: 978-1-59193-223-9
ISBN-10: 1-59193-223-8

61
Gems
on *Highway* MINNESOTA 61

Table of Contents

7

ABOUT HIGHWAY 61

Minnesota State Highway 61 runs
south-north from Duluth, MN all the
way to the Canadian border. Our 61
gems occur along the highway, and
we've given you directions to get from
Highway 61 to each site. For the
purpose of clarity, we're assuming
you're heading north from Duluth
("up" the shore). Each gem is num-
bered sequentially from Duluth; the
higher the number, the farther away it
is from Duluth. If you're coming from
the north, that's no problem—simply
note that lower-numbered gems are
farther south (and closer to Duluth.)

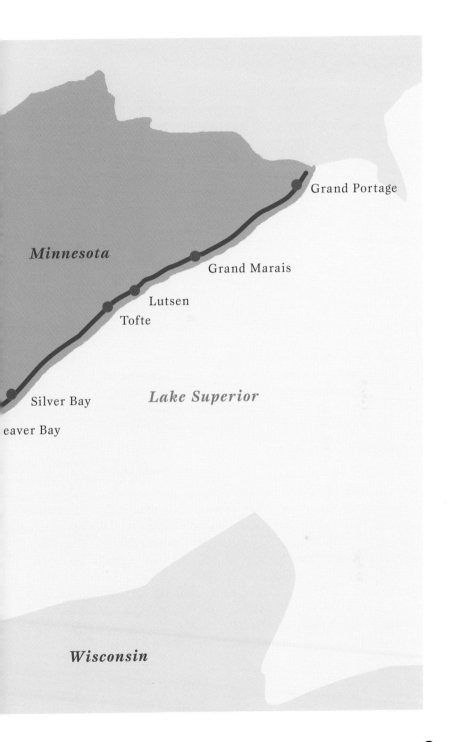

Grand Portage

Minnesota

Grand Marais

Lutsen

Tofte

Lake Superior

Silver Bay

eaver Bay

Wisconsin

9

Introduction

ABOUT THIS BOOK

Highway 61 is renowned for its cliffside views of the lake, the many nearby state parks, and tourist destinations like Two Harbors and Grand Marais. But there's even more here than that—in fact, there are dozens of wonderful sites hidden along Highway 61 that are beautiful, interesting and worthwhile. These are the true gems of Highway 61, fascinating places that are unknown even to many locals. We've spent our lives visiting and cataloging these special places, and during our travels on Highway 61, we have often wondered "where did that name come from?" or "what is that place about?" We wrote this book to try to answer these questions and to share our insider's knowledge with you, in order to show you a side of Highway 61 most people rarely see.

CLASSIC SITES

But some of the well-known sites on the north shore are just too good to pass up, so we're giving you the best of both worlds. We've designated some places as "classic" sites, and there are five classic sites in all. These are some of the most well-known places on the north shore; everyone should visit these sites at least once. We've labeled these as "classic sites" on their respective pages, so check them out. Even better, combine a visit to one of the lesser-known sites with a visit to a classic site—this way you'll see the best the north shore has to offer.

HOW TO USE THIS BOOK

Duluth, Minnesota is the starting point for this book. All of the sites follow Highway 61, and the site numbers in this book are based on distances north of Duluth—a gem with a lower number is closer to Duluth than one with a higher number. To help orient you, we've included the distance (in miles) from Duluth in the top right corner. Of course, this means we're assuming you're driving "up" the north shore (heading north), but if you're doing the opposite, that's no problem either. If you're driving south, a lower gem number simply means that a site is farther south. Finally, we want you to use this book as a field guide to Highway 61, as a quick and easy reference for the ride. But don't overplan; instead, see what happens as the road unfolds.

HIGHWAY 61 AND THE LAKE

As Highway 61 winds along, the sheer cliffs provide breathtaking views of Lake Superior, mile after mile. Epitomized on Bob Dylan's "Highway 61 Revisited," this famous road once ran from New Orleans through

10

Duluth and to the Canadian border. Though Highway 61 is included in many blues ballads, Dylan wrote a different kind of tribute, one that flowed from the northern reaches of his birthplace, showing the world that the blues highway went both ways.

LAKE SUPERIOR

Lake Superior is the largest of the five Great Lakes and the greatest of the Great Lakes. It holds ten percent of the Earth's freshwater and it is the largest freshwater lake in the world (by surface area). The power and fury of the Lake rivals any body of water; her strength and unpredictability have demanded the respect of mariners for thousands of years. Melville even acknowledges this in *Moby Dick*: *Those grand freshwater seas of ours . . . are swept by Borean and dismasting blasts as direful as any that lash the salted wave. They know what shipwrecks are, for out of sight of land, however inland, they have drowned full many a midnight ship with all its shrieking crew.*

THE POWER OF THE LAKE

It goes almost without saying—the Lake's dramatic cliffs, not to mention its riptides and undertows, can be humbling and even dangerous. Then again, this spectre of danger is part of what intrigues us, what makes us sit up and pay attention. The Lake is also a simple joy; many family picnics, marriage proposals and weddings and honeymoon trips have taken place here, making the Lake a treasure enjoyed for generations.

TAKE IT FROM US

Here are some words of advice from two veterans. Remember to bring along extra clothes, a pair of dry socks, and extra shoes in case the Lake sneaks up on you as you walk along. And always bring an extra jacket or flannel. You are likely to find out that the weather along the Lake can change radically in a very short amount of time. You should expect cooler weather than what the forecast says, or what the temperature appears to be when you leave your hotel. It is often 10 to 20 degrees colder by the Lake and a strong wind off of the water can make it feel even brisker. Be prepared for all types of weather, including fog. And bring warm clothes; you won't have fun if you are cold!

Please also bear in mind that the Lake is as dangerous as it is beautiful; the Lake is powerful and unforgiving. As much as we find kinship with her, we are ever called to pay respect to her power. Slippery rocks, ledges and cliffs should be traversed with caution and we beg you—keep children under your close supervision. Too often we have observed visiting folks who were unaware of the perils at hand let their progeny skip along too close to danger; we want everyone to be safe. Streams and rivers might look appealing on a hot day, but unless you are familiar with the vagaries of a particular waterway, you should stay out and enjoy it from the shore. The Lake herself can have an undertow strong enough to pull an adult swimmer out to sea, and it should not be trifled with if you are uncertain of conditions.

CAUTION—WILDLIFE

Driving on Highway 61 should not be taken lightly either; please use caution and pay close attention to the changing conditions along the road. Deer are an ever-present danger and the best advice we can give you is to watch for them, drive a reasonable speed and DO NOT SWERVE! Swerving cars are liable to end up in the ditch, or worse, running into oncoming traffic. So counsel yourself against swerving. Remind yourself ahead of time because it is instinctive. As terrible as it is to think of hitting the animal directly, the consequences of swerving could make matters much, much worse. If impact appears unavoidable, slow as quickly as you SAFELY can (do not slam on the brakes or you will lose control) and, keeping control of the vehicle, get to the side of the road, out of the path of traffic. If the animal is still on the road, call 911 so that it can be moved.

DRIVING ON HIGHWAY 61—PASSING AND PULLOUTS

Another word about safe driving—there are many pullouts onto the highway that are hard to see, so pay attention as you pull out and be aware of traffic coming from both directions. We strongly advise against passing on Highway 61, even where it is legal. Try to sit back and relax. You are on vacation and the ride is half the fun. It's better to get there safe than fast. If the car in front of you is going slower than the speed limit, they are probably just enjoying the view. And it's not a bad idea to slow down, the wonderful views often give way to sheer cliffs and twists and turns; this is not a place you want your vehicle to leave the road!

GETTING ORIENTED

While driving can be a little dicey, it's difficult to get lost on Highway 61, as the road simply goes north-south from Duluth to Canada. For the purpose of clarity, this book is about Minnesota State Highway 61. For consistency's sake, we measured all sites from the same point in Duluth where Highway 35 turns into London Road/MN Highway 61 (at 26th Avenue East.)

MINNESOTA HIGHWAY 61 VS. OLD HIGHWAY 61

Nevertheless, a few of the sites near Duluth are a bit trickier to find. Here, another highway, St. Louis County Road 61 (known as Old 61), parallels Minnesota 61. Almost all of the sites in this book occur on Minnesota State Highway 61, but two sites (the Old Pump House at Lakewood and the Buchanan Settlement Marker, gems 4 and 5) are actually on Old Highway 61. We recommend you start in Duluth, visit the first three sites, jump onto Old Highway 61 for sites 4 and 5, and then follow Old 61 until just before Two Harbors, where it merges with MN-61. After that, all sites in the book are right off of Minnesota Highway 61.

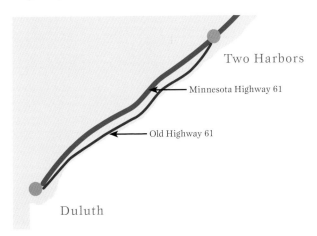

Two Harbors

Minnesota Highway 61

Old Highway 61

Duluth

HAVE FUN!

After all those dire warnings, please be assured that spending time here with your friends, lover, or family will always be rewarding, as long as you are aware of your surroundings, the potential risks, and you are prepared. We hope that our insiders' point of view helps you make wonderful memories, and we hope others will come here, and that they will do their best to take care of the Lake, too. We recognize the spirit of adventure and exploring that will drive you to look for more treasures; it has driven us. And we know the Lake's tranquility can be a balm for a busy life, for there is nothing better than being lakeside. Welcome to the most beautiful place on Earth!

Gem 1 CLASSIC SITE

Glensheen Mansion

HOW TO GET THERE: As you are heading out of Duluth and heading north on London Road, which will turn into Highway 61, the mansion will be on your right. It is well marked. Turn right into the large parking lot just past the main building off of London Road.

ACCESSIBILITY: The main tour is conducted on the lower level and first floor of the mansion; they are wheelchair accessible.

COOL THINGS TO KNOW: No true collection of North Shore icons would be complete without mentioning the mysterious and magnificent Glensheen Mansion. Chester Congdon set out to create a mansion worthy of the ages and reflective of his status as a captain of industry. His home often seems gothic and castle-like today. Money, Victorian opulence, and murder make this storied place definitely worth checking out. Although it is not spoken of openly by today's caretakers (who are employees of the University of Minnesota campus in Duluth) everyone knows what happened here—a notorious murder. Even if you never take the tour or go beyond a glimpse as you drive by on London Road headed for Highway 61, a glimpse is all it takes to look backward in time. Stately doors and windows wrapped in stone and protected by a massive wrought iron fence seem to speak of feudal lords and past centuries. Yet, despite all its grandeur, when

Tofte   Lutsen   Grand Marais   Grand Portage

you step through the grand doors of the Congdon castle, it is somehow warm and welcoming. Maybe it's just an illusion, but it feels like home. You will probably have the same impulse to call out "Honey, I'm home!" when you step into the warm, wood-paneled entry, interspersed with intricate engravings. Don't miss your chance to visit the impressive and brooding Glensheen Estate—no trip to the North Shore would be complete without it.

Stately doors and windows wrapped in stone and protected by a massive wrought iron fence seem to speak of feudal lords and past centuries.

15

Gem 2

North Shore Interpretive Center

HOW TO GET THERE: Just before the Lester River Bridge on the lakeside, turn right into the parking lot just after the big white building.

ACCESSIBILITY: The boat house exhibit in the back is wheelchair accessible, though the main building has stairs.

COOL THINGS TO KNOW: At the North Shore Interpretive Center, many different groups and agencies come together with a common vision; all of them are driven by a passion for this, the Greatest of the Great Lakes and the will to share it with others. With more groups associated with its history than anyone seems to be able to keep track of, its architectural strangeness has often been misunderstood and overlooked. If you stop here, volunteers called "North Shore Ambassadors" will direct you to facilities and experiences you'll enjoy, and they'll answer questions about the building and about the natural and cultural history of the North Shore. Built at the turn of the century as a limnology lab (for lake research), the Interpretive Center has housed many programs through the years, including research groups from the University of Minnesota campus in Duluth, and it continues to host agencies that monitor the effects of watershed changes on the

Tofte Lutsen Grand Marais Grand Portage

Lake and aquatic life. Today it also serves as a gateway to the North Shore, with the information that visitors need as well as information to educate them about current research that is helping to keep our beloved North Shore healthy.

At the North Shore Interpretive Center, many different groups and agencies come together with a common vision; all of them are driven by a passion for this, the Greatest of the Great Lakes.

Gem 3

Brighton Beach (Kitchi-Gammi Park)

HOW TO GET THERE: Just past the sky blue Visitor Center shack and after the Lester River, look for a large brown sign that reads "Kitchi-Gammi Park," then turn right onto a mile-long paved road (Brighton Beach Blvd.) with many pullouts and parking spaces. This will eventually lead to Old Highway 61, also known as St. Louis County Highway 61/Congdon Boulevard. Follow Old 61 to gems 4 and 5; Old 61 joins MN-61 just before Two Harbors.

ACCESSIBILITY: Parts of this area are not wheelchair accessible, but the view from the car is worthwhile and most should be able to access the picnic area and benches.

COOL THINGS TO KNOW: Known to us locals as Brighton Beach, the official signage reads "Kitchi-Gammi Park." Whatever name you use, you will have a pleasant visit. An uncommonly cool spot during summer months, you might find some visitors enjoying the natural air conditioning. In addition to the barbecue areas, beach, and lava flows to explore, you might notice migrating birds passing by. Many picnic tables and benches throughout the area make for a splendid setting for an impromptu meal. "Bella's Castle," another mysterious name, is a small, sturdy WPA (Works Progress Administration) pavilion that may save your repast from the temperamental lake-effect weather. Visitors

Tofte

Lutsen

Grand Marais

Grand Portage

may be tempted to test the waters here, but should be aware the life-threatening undertow. Enjoy the view, though. This is a great place to watch ships moving to and from the twin ports of Duluth and Superior. Try to notice the difference between the "Salties," or ocean-going vessels, and "Lakers," the cargo vessels that traverse only the Great Lakes. While you watch, you can learn a little nautical lingo by calling which way the ships are traveling. Although it may seem counterintuitive, boats headed into port here are said to be "up bound," while those leaving and heading to the Sault Ste. Marie locks are "down bound."

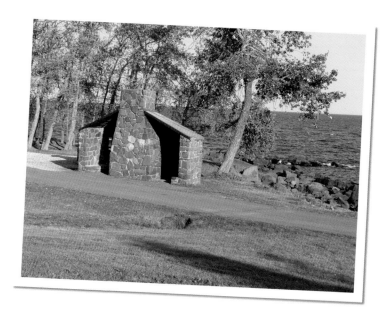

Bella's Castle is a WPA-era pavilion at Brighton Beach.

Gem 4

The Old Pump House at Lakewood

HOW TO GET THERE: Just past the turn-off for the Brighton Beach road, 3 miles north of Duluth, turn right onto County Road 61 (also known as North Shore Scenic Drive or Old 61). Continue two miles. The Pump House will be on your right. Follow Old 61 to Gem 5; Old 61 rejoins MN-61 just outside of Two Harbors. The site's address is 8131 Congdon Road.

ACCESSIBILITY: It's easy to take pictures from the roadside.

COOL THINGS TO KNOW: Here you will find a grand structure. Known officially as the Duluth Water Pumping Station, its architecture is more reminiscent of a castle or a fortress. Still in service, the building was built in 1897 and was powered by steam-driven pumps until 1932. The station provides all the water for the entire city of Duluth, as well as for Proctor, Hermantown and Rice Lake Township. The system is old; many of the pipes have been in the ground for 120 years and some of the reservoirs are from the 1880s. If you could see inside, you would find the original hand-operated bridge crane. Look around and you will find a spigot where you are welcome to help yourself and fill your water bottles with free, cold, filtered water, fresh from Lake Superior! The water you drink can only be had from local taps; thus far, attempts to bottle and sell Lake Superior's water have been resisted. This is also a good place to access the shore for a

Tofte
Lutsen
Grand Marais
Grand Portage

short break. On the little beach below the Pump House, you will be at the spot where the 500-foot steamer *Crescent City* ran up on the rocks during the *Mataafa* Storm of November, 1905. The 1905 Storm led to many shipwrecks and lives lost, though the *Crescent City* was laboriously salvaged.

Known officially as the Duluth Water Pumping Station, its architecture is more reminiscent of a castle or a fortress.

Gem 5

Buchanan Settlement Marker

HOW TO GET THERE: Continue 7 miles past the Old Pump House (gem 4) on Old 61; you'll find the pullout one quarter of a mile south of Knife River on the lakeside, look for a sign that reads "Historical Site." 12 miles from Duluth. To rejoin MN-61, follow Old 61; the two roads merge just before Two Harbors.

ACCESSIBILITY: There are steps leading down to the plaque area. Not wheelchair accessible.

COOL THINGS TO KNOW: A strange sense of what might have been lingers at this deteriorating, yet lovely, historical site. A stone marker rises grandly above the tangled weeds and wild flowers, made more stately by the disrepair and neglect of the benches and small plaza that reminds us that this was once the seat of the United States Land Office of the northeast district. From 1856-1859, the founders of Buchanan (named after the then U.S. President) had high hopes of creating a boomtown, as they believed that there was lots of copper in the nearby bed of the Knife River. With nearly endless white pine forest all around, fur-bearing animals of all kinds, and access to the ports of Duluth and Superior, everything seemed to be in place. Before all these dreams were dashed, Buchanan became a town of firsts: it was home to the first post office on the North Shore and the first North Shore newspaper (the North Shore Advocate, published 1857-1858). Unfortunately,

Tofte

Lutsen

Grand Marais

Grand Portage

the copper failed to pan out and plans fell apart. Shortly thereafter, the land office moved to Duluth. With no reason to exist, it was quickly abandoned and later the empty buildings were destroyed by forest fire. Today it is hard to visualize where a hotel, several saloons, boarding houses, a steam dock, a post office, and a newspaper building would have been. But they were all there. Properly speaking, it could be called a ghost town, but Buchanan is a city of the past, not even the ghosts remain.

Properly speaking, it could be called a ghost town, but Buchanan is a city of the past and completely empty; not even the ghosts remain.

Gem 6

Pierre The Voyageur

HOW TO GET THERE: Follow Highway 61 until you arrive at the small city of Two Harbors. Watch for Pierre on the left side of the road, just past a stoplight, about a half mile after entering town. Pierre is located next to the Voyageur Motel.

ACCESSIBILITY: You will need to pull off the main drag in Two Harbors. You can pull into the nearby laundromat parking lot or the adjacent used car lot in order to get a better view of Pierre. Wheelchair accessible.

COOL THINGS TO KNOW: I can't tell you why Pierre's so cool, but for some of us, he just is. Though Bill raises an eyebrow at this one, I know I am not alone in finding childish joy in the sight of a 20-foot tall, mesh and fiberglass cartoonish statue of almost any kind. Some enthusiasts of roadside sculpture suggest that monuments like this are Americana Art or Architecture. Umm, no. Pierre the Voyageur can hardly be qualified as a great monument to anything, except fun. Built in 1960, he stood guard at the center of the complex that included a museum, which has since vanished, and a motel that is still operating. Back in his heyday, Pierre had lit, moving eyes, a shiny red paddle, and a booming voice that would greet children by name (after mum and dad dropped a note to the man with the mike at the desk of the motel). Pierre would swivel his head, as if interested in the conversation, as

Tofte Lutsen Grand Marais Grand Portage

he answered questions from the travelers in the parking lot. While today Pierre lacks electricity and his shiny red paddle, he has been documented as a historical figure by such prestigious institutions as the Smithsonian and the University of Minnesota. So, show him some respect; he's the last of his kind. Forget that he's just chicken wire and fiberglass; he got here before Paul Bunyan did.

Don't forget to wave!

A monument to fun, Pierre was placed on the Smithsonian's list of historic landmarks.

Gem 7

The Tugboat Edna G.

HOW TO GET THERE: At the third set of stoplights in Two Harbors, turn right onto Waterfront Drive. Follow Waterfront Drive over the train tracks and turn left into parking lot where there is a viewing platform for the tug. You will be able to walk down from there, or drive a bit farther to a dirt track leading right up to the dock.

ACCESSIBILITY: You can drive right up to the dock, so accessibility shouldn't be a problem.

COOL THINGS TO KNOW: In 1896, the president of the Duluth & Iron Range Railroad named his company's new tugboat after his daughter, Edna Greatsinger. Today the *Edna G.* is not only regarded as an icon of the North Shore and Two Harbors, Minnesota, but it was placed on the National Register of Historic Places in 1974. These days she is idled and permanently docked next to the ore docks in the town she served admirably for so many years. In her time, she held many roles: as an ordinary tug for the massive ore carriers in Agate Bay, as an ice breaker, a fireboat, and as a vessel involved in many rescues on the open lake. Her retirement is well earned, though she still stands ready for those with an interest to come aboard and pay her a visit. Proud care-

Tofte Lutsen Grand Marais Grand Portage

takers employed by the Lake County Historical Society will show you around for a nominal fee during the summer, when you can visit the *Edna G.* any day of the week. If you ask, you can blow her whistle, still deep and strong as ever.

The Edna G.'s retirement is well earned, though she still stands ready for those who want to come aboard and pay her a visit.

Gem 8

The Three-Spot Train Engine

HOW TO GET THERE: In Two Harbors, turn right off of Highway 61 at the intersection of 7th Avenue and Waterfront Drive. Follow Waterfront Drive toward the Lake for 7 blocks. At that point you will have reached the edge of town, and you'll see the train depot on your left. The engine will be right next to it.

ACCESSIBILITY: The engine is located just off the parking lot, and the area is wheelchair accessible.

COOL THINGS TO KNOW: Covered with a protective canopy, old Engine #3, later nicknamed the *Three-Spot*, rests comfortably. This noble chunk of iron and steel holds a very special place in the history of the North Shore and Minnesota. She was transported in 1883 by rail from Philadelphia to Duluth. As no rail line existed at that time between Duluth and Two Harbors, the last leg of her voyage was completed by boat. Chained down on a stout barge, she was tugged to Agate Bay in Two Harbors with the help of the worthy tug *Ella G. Stone*. Halfway there, a sudden northeasterly gale blew up, threatening to capsize the barge. At one point the captain told his crew to stand by with axes should it become necessary to cut away the cable that held the barge to the tug; burdened as it was, the tremendous weight of the engine would no doubt have pulled the tug down as well. Fortunately, through skillful seamanship and steady nerves, the *Ella G.* and her captain arrived at

Agate Bay with the engine safely in tow. There the *Three-Spot* began a long and distinguished career. As it hauled the first load of iron ore dug out of the ground of the Iron Range, she was lauded and given great respect. Today the old *Three-Spot* appears as ready as ever to perform her duties. You are free to walk right up and lay your hands upon this piece of American history. And right next door there's even more fun—a much larger engine and the Lake County Historical Society Depot are just nearby.

Today the old Three-Spot appears as ready as ever to perform her duties. You are free to walk right up and lay your hands upon this piece of American history.

Duluth

Two Harbors
Two Harbors Lighthouse
Bed and Breakfast Inn

Beaver Bay

Silver Bay

Gem 9

Two Harbors Lighthouse Bed and Breakfast Inn

HOW TO GET THERE: In Two Harbors, turn right off of Highway 61 at the intersection of 7th Avenue and Waterfront Drive. Follow the brown signs directing you to the breakwall at Agate Bay. Once in sight of the water, you'll notice the lighthouse. Follow the narrow dirt driveway to the garage behind the lighthouse. Reservations can be made online through the Lake County Historical Society (www.lighthousebb.org).

ACCESSIBILITY: Not wheelchair accessible.

COOL THINGS TO KNOW: Imagine yourself back in time, one-hundred years ago, sleeping under the sweeping light of this beacon, in the very bedroom where the chief keeper of the light slept. During the week, you might climb the stairs of the tower to be sure that all was well at sea. If you could do this today, would you? Well, you can! The Two Harbors Lighthouse Inn is open year-round and you could be one of the few people who can say they've spent a night in a working lighthouse. Guests have the opportunity to explore the rich history of the lighthouse firsthand, with a private look into its inner workings. Here you can spend an evening in the sitting room with a keen eye towards the weather and watch over the harbor with a guardian's care. Because of the elevation and the view, the weather and sky are more intense, but this sturdy brick house is reassuringly cozy. And the area around the lighthouse is full of wildlife, a strange

Tofte
Lutsen
Grand Marais
Grand Portage

juxtaposition to the industry of the working harbor. In the morning you can look forward to a sumptuous breakfast served by Lake County Historical Society staff who are knowledgeable about the area and happy to suggest places for you to explore. If you are unable to stay the night, stop for a self-guided tour of the grounds and exhibits. If you do that, chances are you will want to make plans to stay here!

The Two Harbors Lighthouse Bed and Breakfast Inn is open year-round and you could be one of the few people who can say they've spent a night in a working lighthouse.

Gem 10

Two Harbors Breakwall

HOW TO GET THERE: In Two Harbors, turn right off of Highway 61 at the intersection of 7th Avenue and Waterfront Drive. Follow the brown signs directing you to the breakwall at Agate Bay. The breakwall is situated on Agate Bay next to the lighthouse. Even better, the Lighthouse Point trail entrance is here too!

ACCESSIBILITY: There is a wheelchair ramp leading down to the breakwall. The breakwall itself is flat, wide, and easily wheelchair accessible.

COOL THINGS TO KNOW: First called *Wass-we-wining,* or "Place to Spear Fish by Torchlight," by Native Americans, the first European settlers set up shop right here in 1856. At the end of the long parking area you will see the impressive cement wall, girded with boulders, reaching like an arm across the mouth of Agate Bay. One half of Two Harbors (Burlington Bay is the other), Agate Bay's harbor is home to the industries that put the town on the map—the lumber and pulpwood industry, commercial fishing, and the iron ore industry, which has been the biggest overall influence on the area. Iron ore was first transported here by train in 1884. As you walk the wall you will notice Dock #1, closest to the tugboat dock, which, at the time of its construction, was the largest iron ore loading dock in the world. There were once six loading docks here, all built of wood. Smaller docks were also present and were meant for

Tofte

Lutsen

Grand Marais

Grand Portage

goods and passengers, and the shore bristled with the shacks and docks of the local fishermen.

The breakwall itself was developed in stages and extends about a third of a mile into the wide water. A hundred years ago, when it was not connected to shore and was not as large, the lighthouse keeper had to row out to the end to fuel the oil lamp there. Walk on the breakwall in any weather and you will be close to where the sky and water converge.

The Two Harbors Breakwall is an impressive cement wall, girded with boulders, reaching like an arm across the mouth of Agate Bay.

Gem 11

Lighthouse Point Trail

HOW TO GET THERE: In Two Harbors, turn right off of Highway 61 at the intersection of 7th Avenue and Waterfront Drive. Follow the brown signs directing you to the breakwall at Agate Bay. Once you find the breakwall parking lot, just look to your left. At the end of the lot you will spot an arched passageway; this is the trail's starting point. The lighthouse bed and breakfast is right nearby too!

ACCESSIBILITY: Unpaved, but moderately difficult. Not wheel-chair accessible.

COOL THINGS TO KNOW: With little fanfare other than a sculpted arch marking its beginning, you will find this trail to be a hidden treasure that allows you to stretch your legs and meander along the prettiest point in Two Harbors. The path is unpaved and winds along the rocky coast, through majestic cedar stands and past masses of raspberry brambles. You might pause at one of the scattered benches to watch the waves break against the shore, or perhaps you would like to leave the path and cast about amid the ancient lava flows. Either way, you will get the sense of being in a wild area preserved within a stone's throw of the active ore docks and boat launch. The many deer you might spot are not very wary and are used to being fed by guests staying at the Lighthouse Bed and Breakfast. This wild point also hosts fox, rabbits, and

Tofte

Lutsen

Grand Marais

Grand Portage

a variety of squirrels, with the occasional black bear, lynx or moose passing through. We hope that the threat of development continues to be staved off so that we all can enjoy the presence of so much natural beauty so close to town. This miniature ecosystem is unique in its diversity and it supports a host of creatures and plants; nevertheless, it is sensitive to human influence. Log on to www.savelighthousepoint.org to help maintain the well-being of this magical place.

Stretch your legs and meander along the prettiest point in Two Harbors.

Duluth

Two Harbors
Trail of Whispering
Giants Sculpture

Beaver Bay

Silver Bay

Gem 12

Trail of Whispering Giants Sculpture

HOW TO GET THERE: Proceed all the way through Two Harbors on Highway 61 (7th Avenue) just to the edge of town. Turn right into the Visitor Center. You will find the sculpture at the edge of the parking lot.

ACCESSIBILITY: Easy for all to access.

COOL THINGS TO KNOW: American sculptor Peter Wolf Toth presented this impressive work to the people of Minnesota out of respect and regard for its original inhabitants and their plight. Originally created and erected in 1977, the statue was refurbished 31 years later, when the artist returned after hearing from concerned citizens that his creation was falling into disrepair. Unpaid and virtually unnoticed, he set up camp next to his monument and over the course of a few weeks he began the arduous task of restoring and preserving the thirty foot sculpture. Now catalogued by the Smithsonian, it and 70 others are regarded as important works of American art. Without ceremony, Mr. Toth left Two Harbors, and he left the fruits of his labor behind for the American people. With gratitude, we would like to acknowledge this fine work that everyone can enjoy. Toth spent 1972 to 1988 traveling the U.S., donating his time, labor and creative energy, carving a Native American monument in each state.

Tofte   Lutsen   Grand Marais   Grand Portage

He completed a total of 71 statues, including twelve in various Canadian provinces. This entire "collection" of sculptures has come to be called *The Trail of Whispering Giants*. At the Visitor Center you will also find an original CCC (Civilian Conservation Corps) cabin filled with maps, brochures and people of good cheer with good information. They welcome you to use their picnic tables and enjoy their expansive lawn at any time.

American sculptor Peter Wolf Toth presented the impressive work to the people of Minnesota out of respect and regard for its original inhabitants.

Gem 13

Burlington Bay

HOW TO GET THERE: Go through the town of Two Harbors and turn right onto First Street, just past the Visitor Center. Look for the municipal campground signs. In about 200 yards you will see a small parking area on your left.

ACCESSIBILITY: Uneven terrain, but easy for most to access. The sandy beach makes this area inaccessible for those in wheelchairs.

COOL THINGS TO KNOW: One half of Two Harbors (Agate Bay is the other), this bay makes for a nice stop at the water's edge. The tiny town of Burlington stood over this bay for a few years starting in 1856, though it consisted of little more than a steam sawmill and a few shacks. When the bustling pioneer town of Two Harbors came into its own, Burlington Bay was often the site of recreation, boating, fishing, and old-time picnics on the "jumping rocks." If you are ever inclined to swim in the Lake, this would be a good place to do it, with its sandy beach and far-reaching shallow sand bottom. We will warn you that though we have braved the ice-water here, the average temperature is 38 degrees Fahrenheit, with the surface temperature in the summer months sometimes between 40 and 65 degrees Fahrenheit. That may sound warm enough to swim in, but temperatures in the high end are rare and very temporary. Even if the surface is warm, the water just below that is likely 45 degrees, so you are likely

Tofte

Lutsen

Grand Marais

Grand Portage

in for a very short dip! This is a great place to cool your heels, but it is far more common on a sultry day to see the beach's edge lined with people in swimming attire and not one soul in the Lake. From here, you have easy access to the beautiful, paved walking trail. This trail gently rises and falls among old white pines and is curiously sheltered and private, considering how close it is to the road. Nearby you will also find the city campgrounds, with sites for tents and RVs.

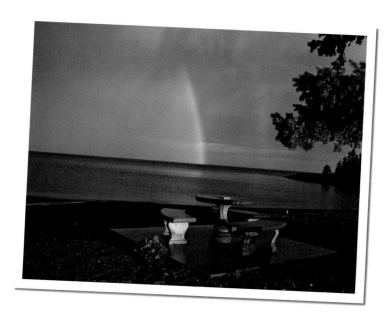

When the bustling pioneer town of Two Harbors came into its own, Burlington Bay was often the site of recreation.

Gem 14

Flood Bay

HOW TO GET THERE: About 1 mile north of Two Harbors, on the right. Watch for the blue sign that reads, "Flood Bay Wayside."

ACCESSIBILITY: All can have a great view from the parking lot, but there are gentle steps down to the beach.

COOL THINGS TO KNOW: Every North Shore beach has its own character, and each visit is a unique experience. It doesn't matter if the weather is howling and you feel nature's power, or the Lake is sweetly rocking and you feel its peace; every visit at every bit of shore is worthwhile. This is particularly true for Flood Bay, a natural harbor with a panoramic view and a pebble beach. The bay was named for a settler who operated a small steam sawmill here in 1856; the bay was an important log landing and rafting site. Today at Flood Bay, you'll often find piles of driftwood heaped up by a past day's storm, and you'll have the chance to search for treasure among the multitudes of tiny agates, always hoping, of course, for that whopper! To find them, try sitting or lying down right on the stones. As you turn over new layers, scan each square inch slowly. Sometimes your best luck will come when you get down close to the layer of damp stones. Agate hunting is good for the soul. It can slow you down and help relax your breathing, heart rate and blood pressure as you fo-

Tofte

Lutsen

Grand Marais

Grand Portage

cus only on finding that whopper. It's a simple pleasure, and even if you don't find any million dollar gems, cherish the journey. Feel close to it all as you listen to the water, feel the shape and weight of each rock in your hand, and discover the joy in such an unhurried, basic pursuit.

At Flood Bay, search for treasure among its multitudes of tiny agates.

Gem 15

Kelsey Beach

HOW TO GET THERE: Located 3 miles north of Two Harbors. Immediately after crossing the Stewart River Bridge, turn right into a dirt parking lot. Kelsey Beach is right across the road from Betty's Pies.

ACCESSIBILITY: There is a somewhat uneven, short path to the beach. Not wheelchair accessible.

COOL THINGS TO KNOW: Follow the path northeast on this beach and you'll find something secretive and special, an area claimed by some to have mystical powers. Visit this beach in any kind of weather and you no doubt will begin to feel the ancient peace that is resident here. This small beach of cobblestone extends beyond the small sanctuary to intriguing formations of stilled lava. Different aspects of this sheltered place reveal themselves at different times of day, but its intimate grandeur is unparalleled at dawn. Skip a stone here in the name of a loved one, or see if you can find the place where it appears that a bear's claw marks have been preserved in fossil form. Look for the tiny rivulets that form miniature falls. Try this: sing something. Together or alone, raise your voice in song and let it join with the great Lake. Offer it up as a shout of joy or a prayer. Something happens here, and it is good. And if that's not enough, visit the nearby Stewart River, which was named for settler John Stewart in 1856 and used for log driving. A logjam once developed near the river's mouth that took three years to clear. You can still see traces of the old splash dams upriver.

This small beach of cobblestone extends beyond the small sanctuary and features intriguing formations of stilled lava.

Gem 16

Silver Creek

HOW TO GET THERE: Approximately 4 miles north of Two Harbors, about 100 yards beyond where the highway crosses Silver Creek, turn right on Silver Cliff Road. Park there, walk back to the creek, and walk upstream for about a quarter of a mile.

ACCESSIBILITY: Fairly rough terrain. Not wheelchair accessible.

COOL THINGS TO KNOW: Called *shonia-zibi* or "Silver Creek" by the Ojibwe, this area was rumored to hold riches of silver ore long before Europeans used it as a logging landing. This is not a designated trail per se, but the area is full of surprises as you follow the meanderings of Silver Creek. One of the delights of getting to know a creek is visiting it in all its different moods, and the temperament of a creek's current is dictated by rainfall. If you stick with Silver Creek, you will pass many gurgling pools and eddies before finally arriving at its first falls, which are diminutive when compared to others, but they are also personal and welcoming, as if the falls were greeting each visitor. Depending on the water level, you can move between the tiny islands and rock footholds, allowing you to make this visit even more personal. There is good trout fishing here during the spring, but when the first rains come and the creek fills with melted ice, the

Tofte

Lutsen

Grand Marais

Grand Portage

creek becomes a torrent. Even if you are not a fly fisherman, you might pause here to catch sight of the large fish moving through the shallow waters, at times leaping or with their top fins protuding out of the water in low pools.

Silver Creek Falls is diminutive but personal and welcoming.

Gem 17

Silver Creek Cliff Trail

HOW TO GET THERE: About 4.5 miles north of Two Harbors, immediately after the Silver Creek Tunnel, pull into the parking lot on your right. You will find the trail running alongside the bluff.

ACCESSIBILITY: There is well-paved trail from the parking lot.

COOL THINGS TO KNOW: At 398 feet, Silver Creek Cliff is the highest bluff rising directly out of Lake Superior. Early roads ran inland, but in 1923, blasting created a dramatic and death-defying road that hugged the outer edge of the cliff. For those of us that remember it, it was the most hair-raising part of an already challenging drive, with plummeting heights and deer herds that seemed to love congregating in the middle of the road. But despite the danger, it was also one of the most gorgeous drives in the country. Since then, this sheer drop-off was converted to a bike and walking trail. Today, the main highway cuts through the cliff itself. The current road is about 125 feet above the Lake; when you pass through the tunnel, which was finished in 1998, picture the remaining 273 feet of rock suspended above your head. According to local lore, a family of feral goats once lived atop the bluff back in the '30s, and when a few local residents spotted a young goat in distress on an outcrop, they mounted a rescue to reunite it with its mother. While the cliff may not

Tofte

Lutsen

Grand Marais

Grand Portage

soar to the heights it used to, every time you pull over here you will be entranced by the grand view. This is one of those rare places that gives that strange feeling that you are standing inside of a postcard, so have your camera ready and record this stunning vista. And if you want a good hike, the Gitchi-Gami State Trail trailhead is nearby as well.

This sheer drop-off was converted to a bike and walking trail. Today, the main highway cuts through the cliff itself.

Gem 18

Wolf Rock of the Superior Hiking Trail

HOW TO GET THERE: Wolf Rock is 10 miles north of Two Harbors. To get there, take a left off of Highway 61 onto Lake County 106, travel 2.3 miles on that dirt road until you find the (marked) Superior Hiking Trail parking lot on your right. Here there is a sweet little path leading up a steep incline but for less than a half mile. The Superior Hiking Trail office is located in Two Harbors and the official start of the trail is just outside of town.

ACCESSIBILITY: Steep and not for everyone, but short. Not wheelchair accessible.

COOL THINGS TO KNOW: The Superior Hiking Trail is a largely unheralded gem of the North Shore and is one of the most comprehensive trail systems in the whole country. Offering mile after mile of unparalleled vistas, it follows the ridgeline above the Lake from Two Harbors and ends near the Canadian border, spanning roughly 225 miles. The beauty of this phenomenal trail is that it provides an endless amount of recreational opportunities. You can take a short hike, enjoy day trips, or make a commitment to living on a wilderness trail, as campsites and primitive shelters are available along the way. There are many ways to approach this trail; you can even arrange for a service to pick you up at the end of your hike and transport you into the lap of accommodation luxury. But if you want a shorter foray, follow us to the top

Tofte Lutsen Grand Marais Grand Portage

of Wolf Rock, which according to the Superior Hiking Trail office is "one of the best spots for a quick fix of the trail." Rising steadily from the parking lot, it might only take you ten minutes to discover a stunning, expansive view of the Lake and surrounding countryside that is guaranteed to take your breath away.

The beauty of this phenomenal trail is that it provides an endless amount of opportunities. You can take a short hike, enjoy day trips, or make a commitment to living on a wilderness trail, as campsites and primitive shelters are available along the way.

Gem 19

Gooseberry Falls State Park

HOW TO GET THERE: On Highway 61, turn right at the brown signs for Gooseberry Falls State Park. You will turn at the first left into the parking lot for the Visitor Center. Located 13 miles north of Two Harbors.

ACCESSIBILITY: The Visitor Center is wheelchair accessible. There is a long well-paved path leading down to a view of the waterfalls. The path is gently sloping but includes switchbacks.

COOL THINGS TO KNOW: If you only have time for one stop on your North Shore drive, make sure it's at Gooseberry Falls State Park. Only 35 miles past Duluth, it has been a favorite destination since the 1920s, when driving the North Shore for kicks began. Since then, Gooseberry has lost none of its allure. With enough to occupy you for a day or a week within the state park's boundaries, you will have access to boundless trails, lava flow formations, lakeshore and river beaches. Explore the awesome Visitor Center or stay in the campgrounds that border the Lake. There are miles of trails and vista after vista from endless vantage points. Again, if you have time for only one thing in the park, do not miss the main waterfalls. They aren't the biggest or most dramatic waterfalls on the North Shore, but they may well be the easiest to get right up next to. If the water levels are right, you will even be able to meander in the midst of the water

Tofte

Lutsen

Grand Marais

Grand Portage

as it trails over long rock ledges between falls. The bridge that spans the river as a continuation of Highway 61 is beautiful from below and gives you the opportunity to walk across the river, right beneath the highway.

*Don't climb wet rocks or let children do so; there are serious injuries in Gooseberry Falls State Park every year. Although there are no fences keeping you out, please exercise good sense in determining safe use of these natural wonders.

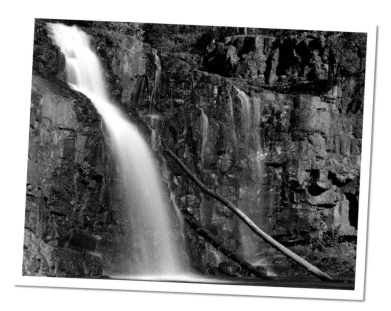

If you only have time for one stop on your North Shore drive, make sure it's at Gooseberry Falls State Park.

Gem 20

Water Tower at Gooseberry Falls State Park

HOW TO GET THERE: Just 13 miles north of Two Harbors, turn
right at the brown signs for Gooseberry Falls State Park.
Once in the park, proceed past the Visitor Center and follow
the signs for the Lady Slipper Building. You will see it on
your right, about 30 feet from the road.

ACCESSIBILITY: There is a short dirt path leading up to the tower
from the roadway and an easy walk for most. This might be
difficult for those in wheelchairs, but it's easy to view from
the road.

COOL THINGS TO KNOW: Encased in red and blue granite, the
water tower in Gooseberry State Park looks like something
from a fairy tale or a mystery from the past. It houses a
10,000 gallon tank built in 1935 by the CCC (Civilian Conservation Corps) to serve the nearby picnic area. With no
well available nearby, workers filled it from the CCC camp
well a distance up river (on the other side of the highway
bridge). In an uncommon move by a public service agency
under severe financial constraints, the CCC program sought
to create beautiful structures that blended architecture with
natural beauty. In this spirit they hired architect U.W. Hella
and two Italian masons to create the tower which would
beautify and cool the water tank. It stands 25 feet tall with a
17 foot diameter. No longer in use, it stands as testament to
what can be accomplished in unity, for the greater good, even

Tofte

Lutsen

Grand Marais

Grand Portage

in the most difficult of times. The stonework of the CCC buildings in Gooseberry includes some of the most distinctive masonry in all of Minnesota's state parks. Of course, while you are there you should enjoy all that the park has to offer. Above the highway bridge there are two waterfalls with a total drop of 30 feet, and there are two falls below with a total drop of 75 feet. There are more than 10 miles of foot trails, a fifth waterfall upstream and even an agate beach at the mouth of the river downstream.

The water tower in Gooseberry Falls State Park looks like something out of a fairy tale or a mystery from the past.

Gem 21

The "Dire Wolf"

HOW TO GET THERE: Turn right at the brown signs for Gooseberry Falls State Park, which is about 11 miles north of Two Harbors. Turn left into the parking lot for the Visitor Center.

ACCESSIBILITY: Accessible for all.

COOL THINGS TO KNOW: The dire wolf, *Canis dirus*, is said to have gone extinct some 10,000 years ago. Considerably larger than the modern gray wolf, it had huge fangs and a powerful chest and preyed on the giant herbivores that roamed North America during the last ice age. The dire wolf is extinct, but in the fall of 1991, DNR officials found the next-best thing. An unusually large and possibly solitary male wolf was making his way from the area of Split Rock Lighthouse and its accompanying campground, when it was killed by a fast-moving truck on Highway 61. DNR officials were contacted to determine what was to be done with the carcass. Due to its near freakish size and the location of its death, State Park personnel were brought in and naturalists of Gooseberry Falls State Park requested that the beast be mounted and displayed in its new interpretative center. But the wolf was so large that the taxidermist had trouble finding a mock body that matched the wolf's size. He eventually had to purchase an Alaskan wolf form, one of the largest, in order to make it fit. Alaskan

Tofte   Lutsen   Grand Marais   Grand Portage

wolves are the largest in the entire world and capable of making a meal of a German Shepherd. Today, you can find this mega-wolf permanently on display inside the handsome new interpretative center at Gooseberry Falls. If you stop to have a look, you will no doubt find it to be majestic and a little intimidating, even though it's behind a glass case.

This mega-wolf is on display inside a glass case in the handsome new interpretive center at Gooseberry Falls State Park.

Gem 22

Belle P. Cross Anchor, Gooseberry Falls State Park

HOW TO GET THERE: The *Belle P. Cross* anchor is located in Gooseberry Falls State Park, about 13 miles north of Two Harbors, Turn right at the brown signs to enter the park. Continue through Gooseberry past the water tower until you come to the end of the parking area. Walk past the picnic area toward the shore.

ACCESSIBILITY: A few steps, but overall it's an easy stroll. Not wheelchair accessible.

COOL THINGS TO KNOW: Once the site of a major logging operation, the mouth of the Gooseberry River has returned to its natural state and is a lovely place to picnic, stroll, or cast a line. With dramatic cliffs on either side of a large sandbar, you can imagine the urgency you'd feel if you had to contend with the 15 foot rollers while trying to find the safety of shore. That's what the *Belle P. Cross* had to contend with. On April 29, 1903, the ship was driven inland by a snowstorm and sank at the mouth of the Gooseberry River. Remarkably, no lives were lost—the 18 sailors stepped right onto the lumber dock without getting their feet wet! Lumber vessels like the *Belle P. Cross* once towed a record-breaking log raft of six million board feet of lumber all the way to Michigan. Making the trip in eight days, the crew brought along carrier pigeons to send for help in case of trouble. We have snorkeled here with the freezing waters of the Lake on one side of the sandbar and the relative bath water of the river on the other side. We found no sunken treasure, but you will find the anchor of this worthy ship high above the shore nearby. Weighing in at about 1,500 pounds, it has a noteworthy history; it once traveled around Lake County in the back of a pickup driven by five boisterous youngsters. Go ahead and give it a heft. Can you imagine moving that huge chunk of metal with four of your friends?

On April 29, 1903, the Belle P. Cross was driven inland by a snowstorm and sank at the mouth of the Gooseberry River.

Gem 23

Gitchi-Gami State Trail

HOW TO GET THERE: Located just 16 miles from Two Harbors at mile marker 42, the Twin Points Public Water Access is a great place to get to the trail. It is uncrowded, with lots of parking. To get there, just turn right into the lot off of Highway 61.

ACCESSIBILITY: Outstanding accessibility, with newer pavement and wide pathways.

COOL THINGS TO KNOW: The Gitchi-Gami State Trail has been in development for years, and the sections completed so far include 21 miles of paved thoroughfare safely away from the cars on Highway 61. The trail was the dream of some forward-thinking individuals and that dream is coming true one mile at a time. Envisioned by the Gitchi-Gami Trail Association as a safe corridor for bikers, skaters, joggers and walkers, a dedicated group of volunteers has helped keep this good idea alive for several decades. When the trail is completed, it will stretch 86 miles between Two Harbors and Grand Marais and will connect five state parks, four scientific and natural areas and several historic sites. It is a good thing to see this kind of tenacity; right now only various segments are completed, but every year more work is finished. The longest section now is between Gooseberry

Tofte

Lutsen

Grand Marais

Grand Portage

Falls State Park and Beaver Bay. Twin Points is an excellent place to hop on, as the trail connects several communities and gives all of us the opportunity to get closer to it all. Visit the Gitchi-Gami State Trail (www.ggta.org) website for more specifics as well as the chance to throw a little support their way for all the hard work they are doing on our behalf.

The Gitchi-Gami State Trail is a safe corridor for biking, skating, jogging or walking along the North Shore.

Gem 24

Twin Points Dock and Safe Harbor

HOW TO GET THERE: At mile marker 42 on Highway 61, turn right into the parking lot, which is well marked. Twin Points Dock and Safe Harbor is 16 miles from Two Harbors.

ACCESSIBILITY: Accessible for all.

COOL THINGS TO KNOW: The Twin Points Dock and Safe Harbor offers a great place to get off the road for a spell. Spacious parking and portable toilets are available, as well as a good place for a short walk. The safe harbor project is geared toward making sensible use of the water and its shore in order for all to have a safe and positive experience. Before the creation of the site, Twin Points had already been developed and later abandoned. On the property that once formed part of the long-standing Twin Points Resort, a safe harbor was completed in 2002 with two ramps and a 150-foot crib dock, providing protection for the launch ramps. The goal was to give recreational watercraft and small commercial vessels safe access to the Lake—a lake with many hazards —and to reclaim a piece of the shore in the process, making the Lake more beautiful and accessible for all of us. Even in ordinary weather, the Lake is unforgiving, temperamental and no place for the unprepared or inexperienced. Between quickly descending fog, divers underwater, commercial shipping and

Tofte

Lutsen

Grand Marais

Grand Portage

the wild weather, there is much a mariner must consider on this awesome, inland sea. Even if you don't have a boat, this is a pleasant place to stroll the sand beach, walk out on the dock, watch boats (which is always an excellent pastime) or fish from shore.

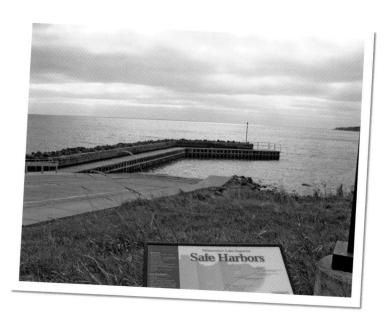

Even in ordinary weather, the Lake is unforgiving, temperamental and no place for the unprepared or inexperienced.

Gem 25

Iona's Beach

HOW TO GET THERE: At mile marker 42 on Highway 61, turn right into the well-marked parking lot. Hike north on the short trail to Iona's Beach Scientific and Natural Area.

ACCESSIBILITY: Not difficult, but not wheelchair accessible.

COOL THINGS TO KNOW: Located between Gooseberry Falls State Park and Split Rock State Park, Iona's Beach is designated a SNA (Scientific and Natural Area). It is named after Iona Lind, the former owner of Twin Points Resort. Iona and John Lind ran their resort here for 50 years; then the family made it a gift to the public as a preserve. It is managed by the Sugarloaf Association and designated an SNA by the DNR. One of the few beaches of significant size on the Lake, this one begins at a northern shore cliff of pink rhyolite and felsite bedrock, and stretches over 300 yards to another cliff of dark gray basalt. This magical pink beach is known for the tinkling sounds the waves make as the flattened pebbles, or "shingles," settle again; listen closely and you can hear the gentle, clinking sound and feel it through your feet. Whether you walk the whole beach, where dark stones are a rarity, or just stand, look, and listen, you will get a sense of the many families that spent decades returning to this beloved spot year after year.

Tofte Lutsen Grand Marais Grand Portage

This magical pink beach is known for the tinkling
sounds the waves make as the flattened pebbles settle.

Gem 26

Split Rock Falls

HOW TO GET THERE: Look for mile marker 43 on Highway 61, a half mile upstream from the Split Rock River pullout/parking lot and 18 miles from Two Harbors. Take the trail heading away from the mouth of the river on the west side. As soon as you reach the first branch of the trail, take a right and head into the ravine.

ACCESSIBILITY: An unpaved path that winds down into a fairly steep ravine. Not wheelchair accessible.

COOL THINGS TO KNOW: This is another genuine gem of the North Shore. Though somewhat diminutive compared to the High Falls or Devil's Kettle, it receives much less foot traffic. This section of the Superior Hiking Trail culminates with a respectable 20 foot waterfall, a lovely wooden bridge and a little forest canyon, a small universe of its own. After making the half mile hike at a gradual incline, the main trail continues onward and a small, steep, somewhat narrow path leads you down to the river's edge and a sturdy wooden bridge. To the left, the falls tumble over a gray granite cliff. Trees and shrubs on either side of the falls crown the water and frame the sky. Immediately to your right, just before the bridge, is the perfect place to have a picnic, as an area approximately twenty feet in diameter lies waiting beneath a cluster of mature cedar trees. Here the river curves sharply to the right and is flanked by a large rock outcropping, perhaps fifty or sixty feet high. The river moves gently against the earthen bank on the opposite shore, and couples will find this place enchanting and untrammeled. Save this one for something special.

On the West Split Rock River you will find a waterfall, a lovely wooden bridge, and a little forest canyon, creating a small universe of its own.

Gem 27

Madeira Pullout

HOW TO GET THERE: To get to the *Madeira* Pullout, follow Highway 61 to Two Harbors. Then continue for 19 miles and turn right into a pullout, just past mile marker 45, which is lined with a stone wall.

ACCESSIBILITY: Accessible for everyone.

COOL THINGS TO KNOW: Take in the only view of Split Rock Lighthouse from a safe pullout on Highway 61 and consider this: When the lighthouse was under construction in 1909, there were no serviceable roads. Everything came by boat and was hauled up the 100-foot sheer cliff. The Mataafa Storm of 1905, which caused the wreck of the *Madeira* (along with 29 total ships lost and 215 lives lost) was the final impetus for the construction of Split Rock Lighthouse. Some of the remains of the *Madeira* lie at the edge of the parking lot; here you can see one bow anchor and a two-ton chunk of the hull. The rest of her lies below the surf, her name emblazoned in yellow lettering still visible on the bow. The *Madeira* struck the sheer cliff of Gold Rock Point broadside and one Fred Benson scaled the 60 foot cliff to secure a line which saved nine of the crew. The last in line, the first mate, was lost, carried down in the stormy waters as he climbed the mizzenmast to try to escape. There they sat on the rocky ledge for two days until they were rescued by

Tofte   Lutsen   Grand Marais   Grand Portage

the tugboat *Edna G.,* which also recovered the mate's body. The wreck now lies in shallow water and is often visited by divers. But you might be able to see it too. If the Lake is calm and the light is right, they say the outline of the *Madeira* can be seen from above. Follow the path behind the old abandoned trading post building to the edge of Gold Rock Point cliff, if you dare, and peer into the depths for yourself.

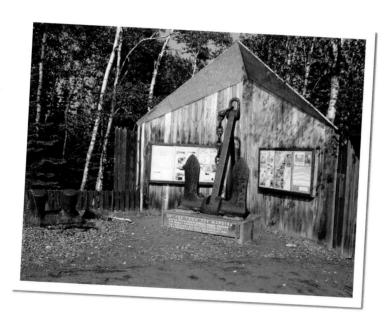

The infamous storm of 1905 wrecked the Madeira and was the final impetus for the construction of Split Rock Lighthouse.

Gem 28

Crazy Bay at Split Rock State Park

HOW TO GET THERE: Crazy Bay is located at Split Rock State Park, 20 miles from Two Harbors. To get there, turn right into Split Rock State Park. After purchasing a permit, park at the most distant lot and head toward backpack campsite #3. Turn left down the hill and follow the small dirt trail all the way down to the water through campsite #3.

ACCESSIBILITY: The unpaved trail is easy, but there's a bit of a climb on the way out. Not wheelchair accessible.

COOL THINGS TO KNOW: Want a hidden view of a popular place? Split Rock Lighthouse is the most visited state park in Minnesota and has been a tourist draw since its completion in 1909, when passengers on the *S.S. America* fawned over it from the deck and demanded photographs and postcards of the high cliffs. When the first real highway was created in 1923, more crowds gathered and claimed it as their own, forcing the ever-accommodating keepers to give tours on Sundays, in addition to their regular duties. By 1936, the park had already welcomed over 100,000 visitors. You might know all of this already, but despite the many, many visits we have paid to the park, we recently "discovered" a secluded and unique beach with its own tiny harbor. Hidden away near backpack campsite #3, you will discover a lovely sheltered bay with rocks of unusual size and coloration, right on the shores of Crazy Bay (we could uncover no explana-

Tofte　Lutsen　Grand Marais　Grand Portage

tion for this moniker.) Crazy Bay is just immediately "south" of Corundum Point, the corundum mining site bought by 3M, which was searching for a natural abrasive. The point provides a great backdrop for sea-gazing, but if the site is occupied, please use good judgment and courtesy when passing by. If it's not, perhaps you'd like to stay for a night at your own private beach?

Crazy Bay at Split Rock State Park is a secluded and unique beach with its own tiny harbor.

Gem 29

CLASSIC SITE

Split Rock Lighthouse and State Park

HOW TO GET THERE: Split Rock Lighthouse is 20 miles from Two Harbors. Follow Highway 61 and turn right to enter the park, which is well marked with brown signs.

ACCESSIBILITY: The Visitor Center and the Keeper's House are wheelchair accessible, but the fog signal house and lighthouse are not.

COOL THINGS TO KNOW: Built in 1910 out of a need made apparent during the infamous and devastating Mataafa Storm of 1905, the Split Rock Lighthouse and State Park now draws tens of thousands of visitors from around the world. For a small fee you can take a guided tour right up to the top of the lighthouse and see the light that shines 20-some miles out to sea first-hand. It is now lit only on rare occasions, including every November 10th, when it shines out as a beacon and as a memorial to the sailors who lost their lives on the *Edmund Fitzgerald*. To witness the lighting of this breathtakingly beautiful lighthouse is a moving and almost spiritual experience. Split Rock Lighthouse, because of its stark beauty and purposeful stance, is a favorite of calendar makers and has even been seen on "Good Morning, America" as a backdrop to American grandeur. It is Minnesota's own Statue of Liberty;

Tofte
Lutsen
Grand Marais
Grand Portage

she is our maritime lady with a backbone. To see it is to know it and to love it. Better yet, you can't take a bad picture of the mighty Split Rock Lighthouse, because day or night, sunset or moonrise, it strikes a proud profile. On canvas or in a photograph, the light dances upon the water and the cliff; this lighthouse is beautiful in any weather and in every medium.

To witness the lighting of this breathtakingly beautiful lighthouse perched atop a rocky promontory is a moving and almost spiritual experience.

71

Gem 30

John Beargrease Indian Cemetery

HOW TO GET THERE: The John Beargrease Indian Cemetery is 24 miles from Two Harbors. To get there from Highway 61, turn left onto Old Town Road (next to the Holiday gas station in Beaver Bay) and follow the curve to the right. Just before the stop sign, stop and park on the roadside. On your left, there are somewhat concealed steps with a log railing and a faded sign that reads "Indian Burial Ground."

ACCESSIBILITY: A steep climb up uneven steps. This site is not wheelchair accessible.

COOL THINGS TO KNOW: Though he died when her mother was just seven years old, the granddaughter of the famous John Beargrease, Vi Keyport, would be proud to have you visit her grandfather's gravesite. She told us that his memory and contribution to the history of the North Shore should be preserved. Immortalized by the internationally renowned sled dog race that bears his name, he kept families and loved ones connected by delivering the U.S. mail throughout the wilderness. During snowy months, his mutt dogs pulled a mail-laden sled; at other times he took to the Lake, and later used a horse and wagon when a rough trail was opened. His father came to Beaver Bay from Cass Lake, but his descendents are proud enrollees of the Grand Portage Band of Ojibwe. His living family admits that he had his own personal struggles, but they also point out that he was a vibrant man that was welcomed at any door. The culmination of John Beargrease's service came with his final act of grand heroism. He died at Grand Portage in 1910 after rescuing another man in distress on the Lake. He was said to have died soon after due to exposure and a bout of "consumption." There are no individual headstones here, so step lightly. Be sure to read the names listed on the Lake County Historical Marker, and remember this inspiring man who endured many hardships and who brought news to so many.

This Lake County Historical Marker, placed in 1932, marks the names of Indians buried there, including John Beargrease.

Duluth

Two Harbors

Beaver Bay

Silver Bay

Silver Bay Marina,
Safe Harbor

Gem 31

Silver Bay Marina, Safe Harbor

HOW TO GET THERE: Silver Bay Marina and Safe Harbor is 4 miles north of Beaver Bay. Immediately after East Beaver Bay, turn right at the signs.

ACCESSIBILITY: Easily accessible, but the road to the marina includes a quick turn, which can be dicey at times, so use caution. The road also experiences a high volume of traffic throughout the summer months.

COOL THINGS TO KNOW: This full-service marina and safe harbor is relatively new to the North Shore. Completed in 1999, it boasts 108 slips, as well as showers, bathrooms, laundry facilities, and concessions. The main marina building includes a sweeping deck with tables and chairs. The grounds also include a scenic overlook at the end of a short trail. Here you can watch the massive ore carriers entering, loading, and departing from North Shore Mining's nearby docks. There are scattered picnic areas, some of which are sheltered, a small beach, and plenty of parking. For scuba divers, the wreck of the *Hesper* lies halfway down the northeastern side of the breakwater in relatively shallow water. The *Hesper* sunk in the infamous Mataafa Storm of 1905. The marina is also a popular and productive fishing location; anglers often catch lake trout and salmon not far from the marina. Several sculptures are scattered through-

Tofte Lutsen Grand Marais Grand Portage

out the marina and add to the experience. All in all, the marina has something for everyone to enjoy, especially day trippers, picnickers and boaters. The overflow parking lot includes a short trail that leads to a nice overlook of the marina and the working shoreline of the taconite plant. Choose this path for the best view of the ore boats being loaded here. Even without a boat of your own, the marina is a great place to boat watch, which is the next best thing to being on one!

All in all, the marina has something for everyone to enjoy, especially day trippers, picnickers and boaters.

Gem 32

Rocky Taconite

HOW TO GET THERE: Rocky Taconite is located 4 miles north of Beaver Bay. Turn left into the town of Silver Bay on County Road 5 and follow it for one block; the statue is on the right.

ACCESSIBILITY: Accessible for everyone.

COOL THINGS TO KNOW: Rocky Taconite is a small monument to the taconite industry that, for better or worse, has shaped the cultural landscape around here for the past 100-plus years. Rocky is a chipper, photogenic, jauntily-posed fellow in black and red and a great example of Minnesotan Americana. Dedicated in 1964 as an emissary for the "Taconite Capital of the World," he wields a pick rumored to have come from old Sweden, a nod to the heritage of the many Scandinavians who settled here and whose many descendents still reside here. Rocky Taconite stands at his post as a friendly ambassador to Silver Bay. The city of Silver Bay was built in 1956 as a planned community, a company town to house the workers at the new taconite processing plant. The geographical location was ideal because of its port and the large amount of water it provided. The town is also an example of the conflicts inherent in development on the North Shore. On one hand, the people here needed jobs in order to feed and clothe their families, but these industries sometimes caused damage to the natural world. But the hardworking local people and

Tofte

Lutsen

Grand Marais

Grand Portage

towns wouldn't be here without that industry. Silver Bay is a reminder that we must make sound decisions, decisions that provide us with the things we need but also protect the environment that enriches our lives.

Rocky Taconite was dedicated in 1964 as an emissary for the "Taconite Capital of the World."

Gem 33

Black Beach at Silver Bay

HOW TO GET THERE: To visit Black Beach, travel 18 miles north of Beaver Bay. Then take the first right past the stoplights in Silver Bay. Veer to the left on the gravel, and drive a quarter mile. Come down the hill past a concrete blender and quarry rock. The road comes to a "T" at the bottom. Turn right at the "T" and continue another quarter of a mile and turn left again. It's just there on your left.

ACCESSIBILITY: The trail is moderately difficult, but short. Not wheelchair accessible.

COOL THINGS TO KNOW: Visiting this beach is a strange experience, and one that might serve as a reminder to us all to tread lightly on this planet. The only black beach we have seen on the North Shore, it seems exotic, especially in contrast to the reddish hue of a nearby island. The beach's dark coloration is not natural, but came about as a result of the taconite tailings that were dumped in the water offshore. Taconite is low-grade iron ore, which is mined on the Iron Range, 50 to 80 miles from here. The ore is refined, processed, and then baked, creating taconite pellets which are small and easy to transport. The tailings are the remnants of this process; tailings were dumped into the Lake here for about 25 years. This continued until locals, especially commercial fishermen, protested. One fisherman said that within a few years water clarity had diminished to "just a

Tofte

Lutsen

Grand Marais

Grand Portage

foot or so" from an original water clarity of about 55 feet. This pushed the herring and other fish miles offshore. Dumping ceased around 1980 and since then the tailings have been disposed of in a land-based disposal basin. The fight to clean up the Lake was contentious; many families depended on the plant for their work and survival. But within five years, the water cleared and the fish returned to the area. So when you visit, keep in mind how we can change things for the better, if the cause is right.

The only black beach we have seen on the North Shore, it is exotic and contrasts greatly with the reddish hue of a nearby island.

Gem 34

Palisade Head

HOW TO GET THERE: Palisade Head is 3 miles north of Silver Bay. To get there, turn right off of Highway 61 at the green sign that reads "Palisade Head," just before the Palisade Creek bridge. Follow that paved, narrow, steep road as it winds up and back toward the Lake. It will take you to the parking lot where you can walk out onto the cliff itself.

ACCESSIBILITY: Extreme caution should be exercised here; there are no railings or room for missteps. It is a short walk to the cliff from the lot, on uneven terrain, and you are very high up over the water. Not wheelchair accessible.

COOL THINGS TO KNOW: Palisade Head is at a pullout just outside of the town of Silver Bay. Tettegouche State Park is the entity responsible for managing this scenic outcropping. Marked only with a modest sign, it is an unparalleled place to stand at a great height and take in the awesome view. An extension of the nearby age-old Sawtooth Mountains, Palisade Head is an outcropping of ancient rhyolite and is not to be rivaled by any location on the Great Lakes. It's almost a sin to miss this panoramic view of the North Shore. Once a land of volcanoes and lava, time and temperate weather have made it accessible to human travelers. Standing here is a sublime experience; you realize your frailty and good fortune to be in the right place at the right time, but don't forget that majesty

and danger stand side by side—you are required to use all
your senses to be safe. Be sure to watch the little ones closely
here; there are no fences or railings to remind you where the
edges are. But this place is worth the risk; it's an excellent
place for a photo shoot, and you will be able to see for miles.
On a clear day you just may be lucky enough to see the edge
of the Apostle Islands across the great expanse of water.

On a clear day you just may be lucky enough to see
the edge of the Apostle Islands across the great expanse
of water.

Gem 35

Trail to Shovel Point at Tettegouche State Park

HOW TO GET THERE: The turn-off for Shovel Point is 4 miles north of Silver Bay at the Baptism River Rest Area. The NE corner of the upper parking lot will lead you to the trail.

ACCESSIBILITY: If you're afraid of heights, this might not be the place for you. In addition, be sure to keep an eye on children and pets here, as sections of the trail are very narrow and there are steep cliffs. Not wheelchair accessible.

COOL THINGS TO KNOW: The trail to Shovel Point is an hour-long round trip and strenuous at times, but it's worth the effort, as you'll be rewarded with spectacular views and stunning heights. The trail is approximately three-quarters of a mile long and follows the Lake for a quarter mile, culminating at Shovel Point, which looks down on the towering palisades of the shoreline. These palisades are reddish lava formations and the cliffs are made up of porphyritic felsite that has naturally fractured into giant six-sided columns. These vistas are within Tettegouche State Park, which was named by the Micmac Indians brought here to work in logging camps at the turn of the century. The accompanying photo shows the awesome view that you will find at the head of this special trail. Here, and all along the way, you will catch different perspectives of the dramatic outlet of the Baptism River, first

Tofte

Lutsen

Grand Marais

Grand Portage

called "Au Bapteme" by the French missionaries, because they used its waters in the baptisms of the native peoples. There is much to take in here, and the sense of being high above it all is spine-tingling, but not for the faint-hearted!

The trail culminates at Shovel Point, which looks down on the towering palisades of the shoreline.

Gem 36   CLASSIC SITE

Tettegouche State Park

HOW TO GET THERE: Tettegouche State Park is 4 miles north of Silver Bay. To find the park, turn right off of Highway 61 into the park, which is well marked with brown signs. You will find the Visitor Center on the edge of that parking lot before coming to the roads that lead to the campgrounds.

ACCESSIBILITY: The Visitor Center is wheelchair accessible. However, most of the other areas of the park have trails that are not wheelchair accessible.

COOL THINGS TO KNOW: Located less than 60 miles from Duluth, Tettegouche State Park is a cornucopia of outdoor experiences for those who want to explore the North Shore. There is an unusual concentration of state parks on the North Shore and in northern Minnesota, and for good reason, with the wealth of natural beauty here. Unlike other parks, Tettegouche has come to oversee, bit by bit, so many stretches of land and shore that it is now designated a "North Shore Biocultural Region." When you enter the main office area, you can go into the campgrounds, park at the Shovel Point trailhead, or go on to cross under Highway 61 and head back inland to another batch of trails. Tettegouche State Park is unique as it even includes several inland lakes and four cabins you can rent for an overnight stay. The cabins are part of what is called Tettegouche Camp and they are on the National Register of Historic Places. These rustic cabins are

Tofte

Lutsen

Grand Marais

Grand Portage

left from the bygone days of a well-to-do men's club that bought the land from a lumbering enterprise in 1910. This is a true forest getaway, as these cabins cannot be reached by road. You have to trek overland to reach them, a journey you will surely find rewarding because of the serene atmosphere. With over 9,000 acres to explore, do not forget to find your way to the 60-foot-high falls on the Baptism River.

Tettegouche State Park is interesting, as it includes several inland lakes and four cabins you can rent for an overnight stay.

Gem 37

Crystal Beach

HOW TO GET THERE: Just a quarter mile past Highway 1 and 5 miles north of Silver Bay, cross the "overpass" for Crystal Creek (marked by a small green sign) and find the gravelly pullout about 150 yards beyond on the right. Scout around a bit and find the narrow and winding trail.

ACCESSIBILITY: There is a steep hike to the beach. The path is difficult and covered with shale. Not wheelchair accessible.

COOL THINGS TO KNOW: Flowing out from the surrounding hills, Crystal Creek is full of beautiful, multicolored stones and the beach itself is truly majestic. Gnarled northern white cedar trees cling to the nearby cliff faces, and the sea caves tucked beneath them seem to shelter secrets or hidden treasure. This is perhaps why the founders of 3M, a company which would later become one of the most powerful corporations on the planet, chose this location to mine for minerals. Here they discovered what they believed was corundum—an ideal abrasive stone—one they could use to mass produce grinding wheels and use to fashion their own variant of sandpaper. 3M even went so far as to build a foundry and dock alongside Crystal Creek. They spent a year mining what they thought was corundum. Finally in the winter of 1903-04 they shipped a ton of the ore to Duluth, only to discover their geologists had made a mistake and the ore was useless. The site was quickly dismantled and abandoned. Such are the unlikely beginnings of a corporate empire. Today the moss-covered remains of the old foundation are still here; they are an interesting diversion as you make your way down to the beach. It's worth the trek, as something about the place makes one dream big. If you're like us, you'll find it difficult to leave this storied place.

Flowing out from the surrounding hills, Crystal Creek is full of beautiful, multicolored stones, and the beach itself is truly majestic.

Gem 38

Illgen Falls

HOW TO GET THERE: Turn left onto Highway 1, which is about 6.5 miles north of Silver Bay. About 1.5 miles up the road turn left after the sign which reads "Devil's Rock." The Illgen Falls trail is on the left.

ACCESSIBILITY: The trail is uneven, unpaved, but short. Not wheelchair accessible.

COOL THINGS TO KNOW: If you've never heard of Illgen City, it's only because you live in the wrong century. At one time, this inauspicious location sported the finest hotel to be found between Duluth and Thunder Bay. The Aztec, in its heyday, looked like something that belonged in Atlantic City, or maybe Chicago. A man by the name of Illgen, its builder, was something of a world traveler and fancied that his hotel had a flavor reflecting the inns of Old Mexico. Built in 1924, it included a large bar, complete with slot machines and expensive liquors. Local legend says Chicago's criminal elite and even Al Capone stopped by on their way to secret northern lodges where they evaded G-men and caught up on their fishing. Take the steep, but short walk behind the cabin (gem 39) and find an Eden-like scene before you. Your efforts will reveal a tall waterfall, impressive even during the drought when we photographed it. The waters of Baptism River fall into a huge, dark pool underneath—a beautiful and glorious sight. Surrounded by huge, round boulders, the falls plummet 30 feet and have been immortalized by a German immigrant whose painting of the falls is preserved on the walls of an antique store in old downtown Two Harbors. Explore the top of the falls if you will; if the water level permits you will find ancient potholes which were carved ever so slowly by the constantly running waters and tumbling stones.

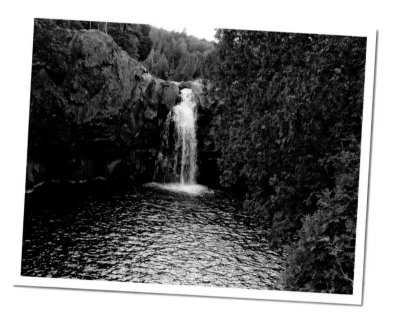

The waters of the Baptism River fall into a huge, dark pool underneath—a beautiful and glorious sight.

Gem 39

Illgen Falls Cabin

HOW TO GET THERE: Turn left on Highway 1, which is 6.5 miles north of Silver Bay, and head away from the Lake. You will find the turnoff for Illgen Falls just a mile and a half up the road on your left, right after the sign that reads "Devil's Rock." The Illgen Falls cabin is right nearby.

ACCESSIBILITY: No accessibility problems.

COOL THINGS TO KNOW: Illgen Falls Cabin is a quaint little building that was once a private residence; it is now owned and managed by Tettegouche State Park. It provides a unique opportunity—you stay within the boundaries of the park with all its natural beauty, and have all the convenience, privacy and amenities of a cabin retreat. There are two bedrooms, one upstairs and one downstairs, so you might make it an intimate retreat, a getaway with friends or fun for the whole family. Though small, the cabin houses a kitchen and a living room with a TV. It boasts a full kitchen with amenities, but you will need to bring your own linens and towels. The cabin is available for rent year-round, and in the colder months you can gather around the gas fireplace for some cozy downtime. Operated by park staff for the last six years, it has been fully re-modeled and is fully accessible for those with disabilities. There are no nearby connecting trails

Tofte

Lutsen

Grand Marais

Grand Portage

to the park's extensive trail system within Tettegouche State Park; however, there is a short trail nearby to the Baptism River. If you stay here, you will be sleeping less than 100 feet from the lovely little falls. Staying here is worth it; spending a night in this cozy cabin is like having a secret lease on the life of a forest ranger.

The Illgen Falls Cabin provides a unique opportunity—you get to stay within the boundaries of a state park and have all the convenience, privacy and amenities of a cabin retreat.

Gem 40

Taconite Harbor

HOW TO GET THERE: Taconite Harbor is 22 miles north of Silver Bay, just before mile marker 77. To visit, turn right at the entrance, which is marked with a sign.

ACCESSIBILITY: There is a paved parking lot in the exhibit area; other areas are not wheelchair accessible.

COOL THINGS TO KNOW: As you leave Highway 61 and pass along the long drive down to the harbor, you will drive through a ghost town first. The wide, weed-covered open spaces give you an eerie sense of something missing. Indeed, there were once homes here, and a taconite plant, all part of a complete little town. The twenty-four prefabricated homes are gone now, but you can still see sections of the old streets, and a couple of defunct streetlights hang above now empty spaces. Farther down the road, you will pass a display of sorts, the likes of which you will seldom find elsewhere; it consists of heavy equipment used in the iron ore and shipping industries. There are four huge items with signage that explains their functions and history, including a massive scoop and an eight-foot-high tire from an 85-ton dump truck. Two massive anchors are also here; one, from the ore-carrier *Bethlehem*, weighs in at 7,000 pounds. The other, from the *Butterfield*, includes the anchor and capstan. The *Butterfield* was a tug and used as a "lumber hooker" from 1919 to 1957 and spent two years in military

Tofte

Lutsen

conite Harbor

Grand Marais

Grand Portage

service. All these artifacts are a preface of what you came to see—the harbor itself. In order to create a harbor, two natural islands were used as anchors and a breakwall was built between them. Early maps labeled this place as "Two Island River." Once used for shipping taconite, the plant site has now been converted to a power plant. The harbor is now used as a public water access site and a safe harbor.

In order to create a harbor, two natural islands were used as anchors and a breakwall was built between them.

Gem 41

Father Baraga's Cross

HOW TO GET THERE: Father Baraga's Cross is in the town of Schroeder, 26 miles north of Silver Bay. After crossing the Cross River Bridge, look for a small sign on the right hand side of the road. Follow the gravel road to the small parking area.

ACCESSIBILITY: Follow the narrow dirt path a short distance from the parking area. There is a short, but winding, dirt path. Not wheelchair accessible.

COOL THINGS TO KNOW: In 1846, Father Baraga, a missionary priest, undertook his voyage from the far shores of the Apostle Islands on a mission of mercy. News had reached him that the Anishinabe people at Grand Portage were sick. He and his lone companion, Dubois, left Madeline Island in a small wooden vessel equipped with oars and a single sail. The trip of forty miles was nearly undone when a strong storm came up as they were halfway across the Lake. Father Baraga prayed fervently for safe passage and the storm broke. The two arrived safely at the mouth of what is now called the Cross River. The river was named after the modest wooden cross Father Baraga and his companion erected in gratitude on an outcropping overlooking the Lake and the river mouth. Today a granite replacement stands in its place, forever commemorating his brave and honorable voyage.

Father Baraga's Cross

Tofte

Lutsen

Grand Marais

Grand Portage

During the summer months, church services are held at the foot of the cross, and congregants sit on the rock shelf below. It is hard to imagine a more beautiful church than the shore of Lake Superior, which has received the prayers of multitudes from every faith.

Father Baraga erected a modest wooden cross here at the mouth of the Cross River in gratitude for safe passage.

Gem 42

Cross River Heritage Center

HOW TO GET THERE: The Heritage Center is in the town of Schroeder at milepost 79. Located 26 miles north of Silver Bay, it's about halfway between Duluth and Canada.

ACCESSIBILITY: No accessibility problems.

COOL THINGS TO KNOW: A landmark building, completed in 1929, the Cross River Heritage Center is the only example of Tudor-style architecture in Cook County. The original wood floor and stone fireplace are intact. The building has been an inn, a general store and boarding house, among other things. Recently renovated and run by the Schroeder Area Historical Society, the Heritage Center is dedicated to preserving and sharing the cultural history of the area. Their gift shop is exceptional and carries regional artwork by artisans who live in the area. Their exhibits of photographs, memorabilia and artifacts of early pioneer days are fun to look through and it's always interesting to place yourself in the shoes of a pioneer and try to imagine what you would have had to endure "back then." One of the Center's primary goals is to educate visitors about the architecture of renowned architect Edwin Lundie. From the 1940s through the 1960s, Lundie designed and built seventeen cabins and summer homes along an 80 mile stretch of the North Shore. The Cross River Heritage Center documents his work and offers annual tours of a selection of these buildings, all of which benefited from Lundie's devotion

Tofte
Lutsen
Cross River
Heritage Center
Grand Marais
Grand Portage

to detail and love of fine craftsmanship. Lundie drew heavily from Scandinavian influences—incorporating carved pillars, and heavy, visible timbers. The Cross River Heritage Center offers you and your family a chance to step inside the past. Several bedrooms that have been restored to period styles can be toured and leave you free to imagine spending a night at the old Inn in a time when the wilderness was just opening up to tourism.

A landmark building completed in 1929, the Cross River Heritage Center is the only Tudor-style architecture in Cook County.

Gem 43

Temperance River, Cauldron Trail

HOW TO GET THERE: Located 1 mile north of Schroeder. Go over the Temperance River Bridge. Just before the state park entrance, park on either side. This trail is not on the lakeside.

ACCESSIBILITY: The first portion of the trail is easy and unpaved but becomes moderately difficult if you want to climb to the top. Please take children in hand, as there is no guardrail along this powerful river. Not wheelchair accessible.

COOL THINGS TO KNOW: The water of the Temperance River swirls mightily, carving potholes in the ancient rock. Originating from its source in the Boundary Waters Canoe Area Wilderness, Brule Lake feeds this waterway. In its last half mile, the river descends a grand total of 160 feet. To clear up the name of this river—when the river was named it was said to be the only river on the North Shore without a sand "bar" at its mouth. Perhaps it is different than most, however a sand bar does form here at times, and other rivers of the shore have them sometimes, but not always. The Cauldron Trail includes two different trails; a quarter mile stroll or a five mile trip (both ways). No matter which trail you take, you'll witness a miniature canyon gouged out of solid rock. It features a great cauldron that was cut away over thou-

Tofte
Lutsen
Temperance River,
Cauldron Trail
Grand Marais
Grand Portage

sands and thousand of years by the relentless water. The canyon is even grander at its base or from above, if you choose to make the short climb. Every bend of the river offers unique sights—sights the old cedars and pines have been witness to for many years.

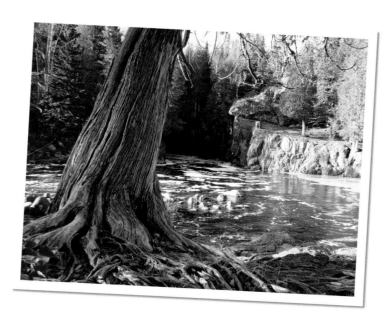

No matter which trail you take, you'll witness a miniature canyon gouged out of solid rock.

Gem 44

North Shore Commercial Fishing Museum

HOW TO GET THERE: Located in the town of Tofte, at the junction of the Sawbill Trail and Highway 61. For details, visit www.commercialfishingmuseum.org.

ACCESSIBILITY: No accessibility problems.

COOL THINGS TO KNOW: Commercial fishing was at its peak from the 1880s through the 1950s on Lake Superior. This great little museum helps bring that history to life and houses many interesting tools and artifacts. The collection includes a beautifully restored full-scale boat from the heyday of commercial fishing, and the many enlarged black and white photos on display here offer a stark look at how difficult life—and even survival—could be in this sometimes unforgiving and isolating wilderness. The museum helps preserve that important story by collecting the stories of the pioneer families that worked and lived here. By documenting the daily lives of these folks, the museum gives us a view into days gone by and a sense of the struggle and tenacity of these hard working people. The fishermen that arrived on the North Shore were often of Norwegian and Swedish descent—countries with a long history of fishing. These men (and women) were fine craftsmen and demonstrated a good deal of ingenuity, as seen in the many tools of the trade found in this worthwhile historical archive.

Tofte

Lutsen

North Shore Commercial
Fishing Museum

Grand Marais

Grand Portage

The North Shore Commercial Fishing Museum offers
a stark look at the reality of survival in this sometimes
unforgiving and isolating wilderness.

Gem 45

Last Chance Gallery

HOW TO GET THERE: On Railroad Drive in Lutsen, across Highway 61 from the Lockport Marketplace.

ACCESSIBILITY: No accessibility problems.

COOL THINGS TO KNOW: Just three years old, the Last Chance Gallery is nonetheless the home of a veteran artist. Tom Christiansen, a cast bronze and direct metal sculptor, heads up this enterprise. His original pieces can be created by collaborative design or consultation, and he uses this working gallery as a sculpture studio and casting facility. Recently heraled on WDSE's "Venture North" as an artist of note in the northland, Tom also carries a wide variety of fine arts and crafts in his gallery, supporting the work of around 50 other local artists. The works range from glasswork, pottery, and fiber work to painting and hand-crafted original jewelry. Open daily May through October, the gallery hosts monthly special events.

85 miles from Duluth

Tofte

Lutsen
Last Chance Gallery

Grand Marais

Grand Portage

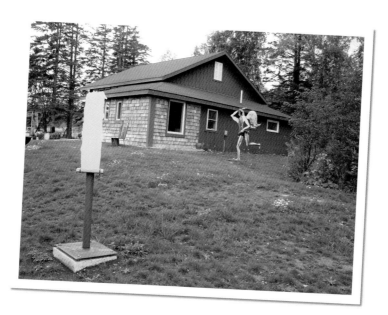

The gallery carries a wide variety of fine arts and crafts, supporting the work of around 50 local artists.

Gem 46

Cutface Creek Pullout at Good Harbor Bay

HOW TO GET THERE: The Cutface Creek Pullout is 14 miles north of Lutsen. Turn right into the parking lot at mile marker 104.

ACCESSIBILITY: Wide open except for the short dip down to the beach. Pathways are paved and extend to the picnic area, but the beach isn't wheelchair accessible.

COOL THINGS TO KNOW: Above Good Harbor Bay is the small Cutface Creek wayside rest, where the construction of the highway cut away into one of the few sandstone beds (overlaid with lava) on this side of the Lake. If you are lucky, you might find thomsonite washed up on the north side of the bay. Named in 1820 for chemist Thomas Thomson of Scotland, this rock is a rare and prized gemstone the world over. Folklore states that Queen Victoria was so fond of it that when it became harder to find on the shores of Scotland, she supposedly commissioned Native people of the North Shore to collect it for her. Most finds are tiny pebbles. You might recognize it by its unique green and pink swirling bands that were formed in pockets of basalt during a single lava event. This six-mile stretch is one of the only beaches where you will find this gem on the North Shore. In addition to the lure of a treasure hunt, this site also has other, more practical, draws. The site is a well laid-out wayside rest and includes benches, paved walkways, picnic tables, permanent

Tofte   Lutsen   *Cutface Creek Pullout at Good Harbor Bay*   Grand Marais   Grand Portage

restroom facilities and a pet exercise area. Those things are nice, but it's the allure of unearthing riches that makes us go back! Spend a few minutes or a few hours exploring Cutface Creek and the beaches of Good Harbor Bay. Even if you don't come away with riches, you will nonetheless be richer for the time spent here.

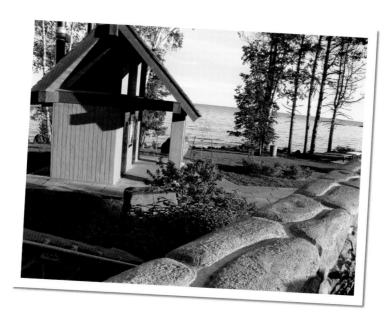

This six-mile stretch is one of the only beaches on the North Shore where you will find the treasured thomsonite stone.

Gem 47

Grand Marais Breakwall

HOW TO GET THERE: Grand Marais is 18 miles north of Lutsen. To get to the breakwall, turn right on Broadway Avenue. At the end of the road you'll be in the Coast Guard parking lot.

ACCESSIBILITY: A bit of a bumpy path, narrow in places and downright precarious if you walk the breakwall itself. Not wheelchair accessible.

COOL THINGS TO KNOW: The Coast Guard station stands on what was once an island, with only some shallow marshy land between it and solid shore. A manmade peninsula now divides the bay and gives you a chance to walk out to a trail that winds through a small, but complete, boreal forest and ancient lava formations. As you stand on those mammoth rocks it's hard not to gaze out at the harbor and imagine what life was like on the Lake prior to the development of modern safeguards and technology. In fact, a shipwreck in 1881 spurred development of the Grand Marais Safe Harbor and Lighthouse. The schooner *Stranger* wrecked just outside of the harbor and beyond the reach of help; all four crew members perished within sight of warmth and safety. Finally, in 1882, the first breakwater and lighthouse were constructed. If you enjoy this place, we encourage you to look up "Harbor Friends" online; Harbor Friends is an advocacy group

Tofte

Lutsen

Grand Marais
**Grand Marais
Breakwall**

Grand Portage

dedicated to protecting the harbor, its surrounding watershed and coastal lands, and the area's natural, historic and cultural resources. Once you walk out onto the breakwall with the Sawtooth Mountains rising gloriously behind the city, you may be inspired to do what you can to help protect such a fine sight.

Before the construction of the breakwall and light-house, the schooner Stranger wrecked just outside of the harbor in 1881.

Gem 48

Chippewa City

HOW TO GET THERE: Chippewa City is one half mile north of Grand Marais. Look for the brown historical marker. Just outside of town, you'll see an old white church on your right. Pull into its parking lot.

ACCESSIBILITY: Mostly unpaved but it's easy walking. There are no major obstacles to wheelchair access here.

COOL THINGS TO KNOW: Unfortunately, we have virtually no documentation from the original native residents about this little city. All that remains to tell us what life was like for them are letters and photographs taken by the European settlers that observed them there. From around 1855 until the early 1900s, a number of Anishinabe families lived here, numbering from around 100 people to as many as 200 by the 1915 census. They were the first inhabitants of this land, but they were forced to adapt to a new way of life by the Treaty of 1854 at LaPointe. Hopefully you will visit the site when the lilacs are blooming, like we did; it makes a pretty picture. Built in 1895, the St. Francis Xavier Church is on the National Register of Historic Places and is all that remains standing of Chippewa City. Still you can probably envision the place surrounded by rough houses and a scattering of traditional aboriginal shelters at the edges. Much of

Tofte Lutsen Grand Marais Chippewa City Grand Portage

the village was destroyed in 1908 by forest fires. The church was saved by the gunship *Gopher*, which was sent by the federal government to fight the fires, but sadly many of the native children died of smoke inhalation. The native people of this little town were known to create beautiful birch bark baskets that they crafted with porcupine quills. They also created beaded bags and other art for the townspeople of Grand Marais and other visitors. This church provides us with living proof of their tenacity and ability to survive.

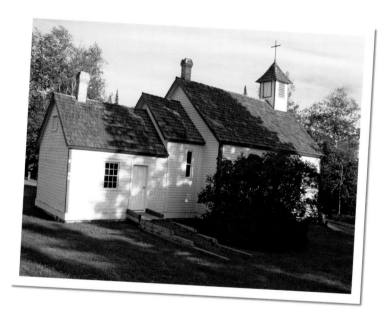

Built in 1895, the St. Francis Xavier Church is on the National Register of Historic Places.

Gem 49

Devil Track River Stonehouse

HOW TO GET THERE: The Devil Track River Stonehouse is located on the north side of the Devil Track River, just after the bridge that crosses the river. It is about 3 miles north of Grand Marais. When visiting be careful and don't stop on the bridge. Instead, find a safe place to pull over!

ACCESSIBILITY: Just look from your car.

COOL THINGS TO KNOW: Now a private residence, this ultra-cool building is a great photo opportunity. Constructed of large stones taken directly from Lake Superior's shore just below, this structure is unique and reminiscent of an old European mill house. Its outer wall lines up with the river's edge and it seems to stand guard over the mouth of the river with all the sturdy determination of a fortress. Doris Croft lived there as a child and her family ran the "Devil's Track Cottages," a resort enterprise that used the stonehouse as their home and parts of it as a lodge for guests. Her husband, Sweenie Croft, remembers when the original building was going up. Only nine years old in 1932, he can still recall local men doing the backbreaking work of hauling the stones we can see now up from the coast. The stonehouse was built on an old bridge abutment, after the old bridge was gone. This provided a wonderful view and some degree of stability. Doris's father

Tofte

Lutsen

Grand Marais

Devil Track
River Stonehouse

Grand Portage

added the upper story and doubled the lower level, and she can recall her younger brother complaining about having to carry cobblestones from the beach for the addition. Doris remembers the lake home as a warm, lovely place, and one with an unbeatable view of the Lake.

Constructed in 1932 of large stones taken directly from Lake Superior's shore just below, this building was the lodge for cottage renters.

Gem 50

Paradise Beach at Colvill

HOW TO GET THERE: The pullout is just north of the Kadunce River, 8.5 miles north of Grand Marais. It starts just south of Colvill and extends to milepost 123.

ACCESSIBILITY: It is a short walk to the beach, but the beach isn't wheelchair accessible.

COOL THINGS TO KNOW: The elusive "Paradise Beach Agate" is known by rock-hunting junkies as a highly desirable stone to own. This long and lonely beach is a great place to stroll leisurely and a great place to relax and burn off all those extra calories you've accumulated while sampling the local fare. Paradise Beach goes on and on, but if you want more, it's close to an entry point to the Superior Hiking Trail. In addition, the beach boasts a historic marker, paved parking and picnic tables for that lakeside meal. Food never tastes better than at the shore in the open air. The lack of superfluous amenities is part of the charm; this keeps the crowds away, and after all, that's what we are looking for in a beach. There is also a primitive campsite and a picturesque cabin, utterly full of nostalgia in its decay. While private development cuts away at the shores, we must cherish such quiet places and do what-ever we can to keep them peaceful and free. Here at Paradise

Tofte Lutsen Grand Marais **Paradise Beach at Colvill** Grand Portage

Beach you will have miles to ponder important matters or let your mind wander lazily if that's what you need. The ongoing expanse of this beach should give you lots of time to reflect, wander, or just enjoy the moment.

This long and lonely beach is a great place to stroll in a leisurely fashion.

Gem 51

Devil's Kettle, Judge C.R. Magney State Park

HOW TO GET THERE: Judge C.R. Magney State Park is 14 miles from Grand Marais. On Highway 61, turn left away from the Lake at the signs for the state park.

ACCESSIBILITY: There is an uphill hike of approximately 1.25 miles, which is unpaved, requires climbing and includes many stairs.

COOL THINGS TO KNOW: The Devil's Kettle might have been called "Mystery Falls." It is said that at the base of the fifty foot falls the water spills into a bottomless opening in the earth. If you ask a park official or local resident where the opening ends up you will be told "No one knows." People have tried to find out by sending semi-buoyant floats marked with paint or fabric to see if they could be located again further downstream or out in the Lake. Thus far, none of these items have ever been rediscovered. Perhaps a series of huge underground caves and tunnels carries the water away to parts unknown. The ancient rock in this area is over a billion years old and keeps its secrets. The trip and trail leading to the small wooden platform overlooking Devil's Kettle is breathtakingly beautiful, especially in fall. Red and yellow leaves mix with the constant evergreens and line the path; breaks in the treeline offer spectacular vistas of the

Tofte   Lutsen   Grand Marais   Devil's Kettle   Grand Portage

Brule River and the surrounding country. Near the trail's end you are met with something of a curiosity—hundreds of wooden stairs that rise and fall, hugging the hills and small canyons, leading toward the trailhead. Frequent rests may be necessary for those not equipped with the lungs of a marathoner. But in spite of this, the hike is tough to beat; a sense of the deep forest and wild nature is everywhere. Don't miss this one.

The trail leading to the small wooden platform over-looking Devil's Kettle is breathtakingly beautiful.

Gem 52

Naniboujou Lodge

HOW TO GET THERE: Turn right just after Judge C.R. Magney State Park. Naniboujou Lodge is located 14 miles north of Grand Marais.

ACCESSIBILITY: Wheelchair accessible.

COOL THINGS TO KNOW: Maintaining a feel for its 1929 beginnings as an exclusive sportsman's club, the Naniboujou is now revitalized, after failing shortly after the stock market's "Black Friday" in 1929. When owner Tim Ramey met with us, he explained how he and his family had come to love the story behind the place and the famous names who signed up to vacation in this wilderness: Jack Dempsey, Babe Ruth, Ring Lardner. Ramey's family strives to preserve it as a place for tranquility and restoration. He welcomes you to stay in one of their 24 rooms and fish or hike the Brule River which is just alongside the property, comb the nearby beaches or just sit on the shore and soak in the solitude in this place. Listed on the National Register of Historic Places, the lodge houses the largest fireplace made of native rock in Minnesota—it took 200 tons of rock to build! If an overnight stay is not in your plans, drop in for a meal in the stunning Great Hall, where the twenty-foot-high domed ceiling and

Tofte
Lutsen
Grand Marais
Naniboujou Lodge
Grand Portage

walls are covered in brilliant patterns of vibrant primary colors. The scene is truly awe-inspiring. The Lodge offers an afternoon tea (sandwiches, cookies and scones) for a unique experience, and welcomes anyone who wants to visit.

Drop in for a meal in the stunning Great Hall, where the twenty-foot-high domed ceiling and walls are covered in brilliant patterns of vibrant colors.

Gem 53

Chicago Bay Gallery

HOW TO GET THERE: Chicago Bay Gallery is 18 miles north of Grand Marais, and a short distance from the western edge of Chicago Bay, opposite the Lake in Hovland.

ACCESSIBILITY: There are stairs leading into the gallery. The site isn't wheelchair accessible.

COOL THINGS TO KNOW: The town of Hovland is a wealth of history and beauty. And whether you are a transplant or a member of a new generation, many try to find a way to live on the North Shore; given how difficult life here can be, this shows a real dedication to living out a dream. The Chicago Bay Gallery is a good example of this; it is an outpost of eclectic curiosities. It features a wide variety of art, ranging from deerskin gloves and bone art made from various animal skulls, to antlers and deer clavicles nailed to a tall post in the yard in a chaotic mishmash of peculiar reverence. These displays of discarded antlers, skulls and other bones cause you to consider again what it was that Georgia O'Keefe found so enigmatic about the curve and shadows of bones. We imagine that whoever found these examples lying amid moss and old leaves felt that thrill that all treasure seekers know, for these treasures were consigned to disappear rapidly had

123 miles from Duluth

Grand Marais

Chicago Bay Gallery

Grand Portage

they not been saved here; the small rodents of the forest make short work of them. Inside you will find many pieces of art to wonder over and to purchase. The gallery features only the work of local artists and artisans.

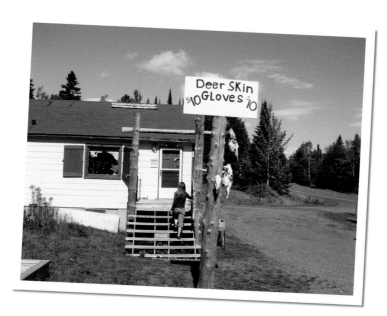

The Chicago Bay Gallery is an outpost of eclectic curiosities; it features a wild variety of art, ranging from deerskin gloves and bone art, to antlers and deer clavicles nailed to a tall post in a chaotic mishmash of peculiar reverence.

Gem 54

Hovland Dock at Chicago Bay

HOW TO GET THERE: Hovland Dock is 18 miles north of Grand Marais. Follow Highway 61, then turn right onto Chicago Bay Road. Travel less than a quarter mile to the lakeshore and you'll see the dock on your right.

ACCESSIBILITY: Pull up to it and take pictures; it's an easy stroll to the dock end. Exercise caution if you venture out farther, as parts of the concrete dock are falling away. The dock is not wheelchair accessible.

COOL THINGS TO KNOW: For such a little and apparently unobtrusive site, this location is rich with history and neat things to see. The old village of Hovland lingers on, and though diminished, it is somehow evident that the heartbeat of the community was a strong one. The dock itself, massive and built for deepwater off-loading, was built in 1905 as the hub of transportation for the packet and passenger ships that came once a week with goods, mail and passengers. Even back then, Hovland was an early tourist draw, thriving with stores, a school and lodging accommodations, though the only things left operating now are a post office and a few homes. With commercial fishing and logging as the mainstays of economic stability, the town was once thriving as lake trout and herring were taken by the boatload. At the end of the dock you can

Tofte
Lutsen
Grand Marais
Hovland Dock at Chicago Bay
Grand Portage

still see evidence of the tracks put in to move heavy crates of fish to a warehouse on shore. The bell that you see at the foot of the dock was rung to signal a ship's arrival and must have stirred up folks on shore with excitement. There are old cottages near the dock that once housed working families. See also the historical marker commemorating the "Old Dog Trail," the trek of John Beargrease and others that stopped at Hovland.

The massive dock was built in 1905 for deep water packet and passenger ships that came once a week.

Gem 55

Two-Fish-House Beach

HOW TO GET THERE: Two-Fish-House Beach is 34 miles north of Grand Marais. To get there, turn right between mile markers 139-140.

ACCESSIBILITY: A moderate walk, but not wheelchair accessible.

COOL THINGS TO KNOW: This is a beach that features a sweeping grandeur; here it is secluded and stately, and a true gem in that it is undiscovered and almost entirely unknown. The deteriorating fish houses are a few of the memorials to the men and families that worked here to survive, their hardscrabble lives now elevated to romantic status. In their desire for independence and self-sufficiency they often found a way to carve out a niche, surviving because of their resourcefulness and inherent toughness. However, it was a hard life with pennies to the pound for their dangerous and definitely unromantic work on shore—cleaning and hauling their catch. Stroll this beach at a leisurely pace; search for the rare lichens that live here, and reflect on how we all are called to do our piece to keep these rare places pristine for those who will come after us. And as you stand here and look far across the wide, wild water, remember that Lake Superior is connected to the Atlantic Ocean by the St. Lawrence Seaway, and try to put yourself in the settlers' shoes, half a world away from Europe and the homelands they left behind.

Tofte   Lutsen

Grand Marais

Grand Portage

Two-Fish-House Beach

This is a beach that features a sweeping grandeur. This place is both secluded and stately.

Gem 56

Hollow Rock Resort

HOW TO GET THERE: Hollow Rock Resort is 6.3 miles north of Reservation River and 36 miles from Grand Marais; turn right at the sign that reads, "Hollow Rock Resort."

ACCESSIBILITY: Easily enjoyed by all. Some of the cabins are wheelchair accessible.

COOL THINGS TO KNOW: This small cabin resort is owned and operated by the Grand Portage Band of Ojibwe and is open year-round. There are six cabins, some of them large enough to accommodate a large group. This 12-acre resort encompasses a small, but beautiful, stretch of the shoreline. We spent a night here in the cabin farthest out on the point; it was close to safety, but separate from the world of human chaos. Then in the daylight we explored what felt like our own private tiny peninsula, discovering the thrones and tables the Lake leaves after thousands of years of scouring at every beach. This leaves each beach with its own character, and exploring them renews the sense of discovery one has in the presence of the great Inland Sea. All of this happened before we explored the Hollow Rock itself, which is close enough to shore for one to reach it without getting their feet too wet. We climbed to its

Tofte

Lutsen

Grand Marais

Grand Portage
Hollow Rock Resort

peak and stood beneath its arch; it's big enough for a small canoe or kayak to navigate. No matter what temper you may find her in, the myriad moods of the Lake are always beautifully framed by the Hollow Rock.

The myriad moods of the Lake, no matter what temper you may find her in, are always beautifully framed by the Hollow Rock.

Gem 57

Grand Portage Marina and Campground

HOW TO GET THERE: In the town of Grand Portage, turn right off of Highway 61. Signs will direct you to the casino and hotel. This is the same road that brings you to the marina and campground. You will need to make a left turn after passing the new gas station/trading post. This will bring you into the marina and campground area; the main office is located on the west side of the marina.

ACCESSIBILITY: Easily accessible to all motorized traffic, it lies in a large, flat area and has easy walking surfaces.

COOL THINGS TO KNOW: While visiting or staying at the Grand Portage Marina and Campground, you will be treated to a nice view of the Lake, and on clear days you can easily see the silhouette of Isle Royale, twelve miles distant. The marina, though small, has character. Surrounded by a wooden boardwalk, small fishing boats used by Native American fisherman are readily visible. The entire Grand Portage area possesses a timeless and an old-world feel. Whether staying in an RV, or a tent, as we did, you can know that voyageurs and the Native Anishinabe people have used the same ground to bivouac and camp for years. Any artifacts chanced upon should be given to a tribal representative or brought to the staff at Grand Portage National Monument located nearby.

Tofte Lutsen Grand Marais Grand Portage
Grand Portage Marina and Campground

During our stay we were awakened in the early morning hours by the whistles and soft grunts of a family of otters, no doubt drawn by the ample smells of fresh fish. They entered the marina mouth like a small flotilla of boats, investigated a few locations on the boardwalk, found little, and left as they had arrived: chirping and whistling, off to other adventures.

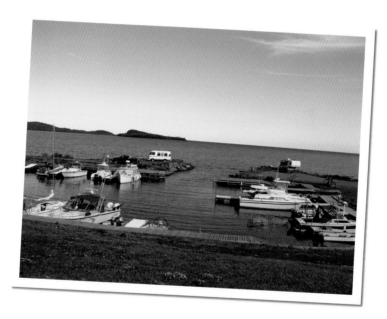

The entire Grand Portage area possesses a timeless and an old-world feel.

Gem 58

Grand Portage National Monument Heritage Center

HOW TO GET THERE: Turn right just before the Grand Portage gas station, then left at the four-way stop onto Mile Creek Road. Travel just a quarter mile farther. The monument will be on your left; it is 39 miles north of Grand Marais.

ACCESSIBILITY: Fully accessible. Wheelchair accessible.

COOL THINGS TO KNOW: The National Park Service and the Grand Portage Band of Ojibwe have joined efforts to maintain and operate Grand Portage National Monument. The new, multi-million dollar Heritage Center opened in 2007 to help visitors understand and interpret this valuable site. Together, the two entities run a summer mentoring program for Grand Portage youth, maintain the cultural and historical accuracy of the information shared with visitors, and preserve Native artifacts and art. Renowned painter Carl Gawboy, of the Bois Forte Band, has prominent work here, along with photographer Travis Novitsky, of the Grand Portage Band. The building itself is a work of art, sitting on the side of a rocky hill with statuesque pillars of raw pine set in the four cardinal directions; the architecture inside and out reflects the circle of life. Its galleries and exhibits feature the Ojibwe culture, the fur trade, a bookstore, multimedia programs, park offices, archives and classrooms. The center is open year-round and is the

Tofte   Lutsen

Grand Marais

Grand Portage
Grand Portage
National Monument
Heritage Center

gateway to the fort that it overlooks just below. The Heritage
Center is an excellent resource for learning about
a critical aspect of Minnesota's history.

The Grand Portage National Monument Heritage
Center houses fur trade exhibits, maintains the cultural
and historical accuracy of information shared with
visitors, and preserves many Native American artifacts.

Gem 59

Grand Portage National Monument

HOW TO GET THERE: The Grand Portage National Monument is 39 miles north of Grand Marais. It's just past the Heritage Center on the right, on Mile Creek Road.

ACCESSIBILITY: Unpaved but wheelchair accessible.

COOL THINGS TO KNOW: Consider this: The arrival of French explorers to this area predates the landing of the Mayflower at Plymouth Rock in 1620. Coming to this very spot they likely would have found the ancestors of the Grand Portage Ojibwe using this fortuitous location to link their summer homes at Lake Superior to winter camps inland. Lest you think that is all in the past, know that there are still Native people in the area following in their ancestors' footsteps— tapping maple trees on the ridge above in the spring, and harvesting fish from the bay below. The fort now welcomes you to take a peek into the way that life was conducted when this was the center of operations for the North West Company and the hub of the fur trade. Costumed interpreters do an excellent job sharing their knowledge and you can visit with them in the stockade, the kitchen, the great hall and a warehouse. One of our favorites was the Historic Garden where a Three Sisters trio of corn, beans and squash flourished. If you are feeling energetic, you might take on the

Tofte Lutsen Grand Marais Grand Portage National Monument Grand Portage

Portage itself—the eight and a half mile trek from here to the remains of Fort Charlotte in the west. The trail rises some 600 feet from the shore and should give you a rough idea of what the original people and voyageurs endured to get to where they needed to go.

The fort welcomes you to take a peek into the way that life was conducted when this was the center of fur trade operations for the North West Company.

Gem 60

Ryden's Border Store

HOW TO GET THERE: Ryden's Border Store is a half mile south of the Canadian border, and 5 miles north of Grand Portage. To get there, turn left into the parking lot.

ACCESSIBILITY: You can all get to this one!

COOL THINGS TO KNOW: It's hard to describe to you how important this last bastion of American consumerism will feel to you as you feel the remoteness of these northern hinterlands seeping into your consciousness. Sure, you came here for just that reason; to get away from the noise and the hassle of the city, you came to search for peaceful tranquility in far-away places where retail stores and fast food chains can't survive. Still, you begin to realize, sadly, how nice it is to get a cold soda, fill up the gas tank or just frivolously spend a few dollars on corny souvenirs. Hence your relief and excitement when you see the sign for the Ryden's complex of post office, café, motel, gas station and (ooooh, best of all) their duty-free shop. Run by yet another generation of the family after 60 years, this is a good place to look around, even if you just want a new T-shirt. We are here to tell you (from Bill's personal experience), you haven't got any idea how isolating, how ultimately "in the bush" you are until you have lived up here. For all its glory and all its loneliness,

Tofte Lutsen Grand Marais Grand Portage Ryden's Border Store

you will feel like you are at the end of the world. Ryden's Border Store at the Minnesota side of the Canadian border is an iconic representation of the lonely outpost. Years ago, when the border crossing was a few miles west of here, the Ryden's had a store there and tiny cabins for rent.

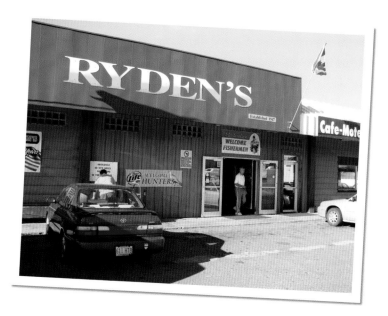

For all its glory and all its loneliness, you will feel like you are at the end of the world.

Gem 61

High Falls of Pigeon River at Grand Portage State Park

HOW TO GET THERE: Proceed north on Highway 61 until you spot the U.S.-Canadian Border; just short of the border, there will be a sign indicating that a sharp left-turn is required if you wish to observe the famous falls. 5.5 miles north of Grand Portage, ½ mile past Ryden's Store.

ACCESSIBILITY: After approximately a half mile, the path culminates in a series of sturdy wooden boardwalks that fork at the end, providing hikers with two viewing platforms, one of which is handicap accessible.

COOL THINGS TO KNOW: It is unlikely that you will find your journey to the High Falls to be a crowded one. When we visited the falls in late August, we saw only three other people climbing their way to the lookout. The area has a lonely and far-away feel to it; no wonder that the voyageurs considered it a rite of passage to have made the steep and arduous journey up *le grand portage*. For well over 200 years these men of the north carried on their backs the treasures of the New World, bound for the greatest cities of Europe. Beaver pelts were nearly worth their weight in gold, and the price of a fine beaver fur hat in the first part of the 19th century was roughly equivalent to the price of a new car today. A typical voyageur was a small, compact man, not more than five feet, six inches

Tofte

Lutsen

Grand Marais

Grand Portage

High Falls of Pigeon
River at Grand Portage
State Park

tall. They drank and sang their way across North America, often carrying two 90 pound packs over treacherous terrain, in this case to avoid the High Falls. So while you huff and puff your way through to the falls, imagine taking on the entire portage while carrying 180 pounds on your back, hungover and ill-fed to boot! The falls themselves are spectacular at 120 feet, and are, in fact, the highest the state of Minnesota has to offer, though shared as a border with Canada.

The area has a lonely and far-away feel to it, no wonder the voyageurs considered it a rite of passage to make the steep and arduous journey up "le grand portage"

About the Authors

Bill Mayo is a former Duluth resident and has lived in Two Harbors, Minnesota, for the last twenty-three years. Long a part of the poetry scene of the North Shore and a former Artist-in-Residence for Isle Royale National Park, he has published work in *National Geographic's Traveler, Poets Who Haven't Moved to St. Paul* and *Zenith City Arts*. He also holds an AAS Degree in Human Services and is an enrolled mem- ber of the Leech Lake Pillager Band. His love of the North Shore came early while driving along old Highway 61 with his parents as a boy. Whether in a canoe, diving or walking the beach, the eternal mystery of the Lake is always awe-inspiring for him.

A Minnesota native and longtime visitor to the North Shore, Kate Mayo now resides within view of Lake Superior. Frequent trips "Up North" finally gave over to permanent residence, and Kate has drawn on her previous perspective as a visitor to the area in the compilation of these narra- tives. She spent most of her career in the role of counselor and is a licensed therapist and addictions counselor with an MA in counseling psychology.